YOUR CALLING AS A BROTHER

YOUR CALLING AS A BROTHER

Brother EDWARD L. CASHIN, F.M.S., M.A., Ph.D.

RICHARDS ROSEN PRESS, INC., NEW YORK 10010

NIHIL OBSTAT: John A. Goodwine, J.C.D.
Censor Librorum

IMPRIMATUR: ✠ Terence J. Cooke, V.G.

December 1, 1965

The nihil obstat and imprimatur are official declarations that a book or pamphlet is free of doctrinal or moral error. No implication is contained therein that those who have granted the nihil obstat and imprimatur agree with the contents, opinions or statements expressed.

Library of Congress Catalog Card Number 66-12894

Published in 1966 by Richards Rosen Press, Inc.
29 East 21st Street, New York City, N.Y. 10010

FIRST EDITION

Manufactured in the United States of America

About the Author

Bro. Edward Cashin was born July 22, 1927, in Augusta, Georgia. He attended the high school conducted by the Marist Brothers, graduating in 1945. He began study as a Marist Brother in Poughkeepsie, New York, that year.

In 1949, Bro. Edward was appointed to Mount St. Michael Academy, Bronx, New York. The principal subject taught by him during ten years there was American History. In 1958, he received an award from the Freedom Foundation, at Valley Forge. His major extracurricular interest was in public speaking. He served as President of the New York Catholic Forensic League and member of the Executive Committee of the National Catholic Forensic League.

Meanwhile, Bro. Edward continued his graduate studies in American History at Fordham University, receiving an M.A. in 1956 and a Ph.D. in 1962. From 1959 to 1962 he taught at Christopher Columbus High School, Miami, Florida, serving as assistant principal during part of that time. While there, he organized the Catholic Forensic League of Miami, and hosted the national finals in 1962.

Bro. Edward was appointed to the faculty of Marist College in Poughkeepsie upon his return from a semester of study in Fribourg, Switzerland. In August of 1963, he was named academic vice-president of the College. During the fall of 1964, while the president of the College Bro. Linus Foy was in Europe, Bro. Edward served as acting president.

For the past year, Bro. Edward has headed a committee charged with the task of studying the life of the modern teaching brother, and the problems of adaptation in that life.

Table of Contents

Introduction 9

I. *Monastic Brothers: From the Solitaries to the Mendicants* 15
II. *Teaching Brothers: From the Brothers of the Common Life to the Brothers of the Christian Schools* 27
III. *Modern Orders Emerge: Nineteenth Century France Produces the New Teaching Communities* 36
IV. *The Secular Institutes: A New Form of Religious Life Among the Old* 47
V. *The American Tradition: In Colonial America Few Brothers, But Much Brotherhood* 55
VI. *The Great Migration: European Brotherhoods Graft on to the American Tradition* 63
VII. *The Great Migration: How One Order Made the Crossing* 72
VIII. *Responding to the Call: How Men Decide to Become Brothers* 76
IX. *Becoming a Brother: What the Training Is Like* 86
X. *Becoming a Brother: An Autobiography* 90
XI. *Brothers in the Future: Where Are They Going?* 105
XII. *The Converging Brotherhoods: A Lesson for Our Times* 123

Appendix 132

Bibliography 156

Your Calling as a Brother

Brotherhood is a human ideal. At all times some deep-rooted impulse has caused men to band together in pursuit of a common goal. The *comitatus* of the Germanic tribes, the guild of the medieval tradesmen, the joint-stock companies which colonized America, the town meetings of New England, the Sons of Liberty of the Revolution, the secret societies and not-so-secret fraternal organizations, the college fraternities and trade union brotherhoods—all are bits and pieces of evidence that men are instinctively joiners. The important things are done by well-organized and capably led groups of men. The pattern is of a piece: a thinker discovers a need in society and points a way to its solution; an entrepreneur assembles the machinery of organization; individuals whose talents and inclinations fit them for the work join together. Those recognized by history as the greatest individuals are those who have put together the greatest organizations.

In our time, this rugged individualist has been replaced by the organization man. The frontiers are gone and men are crowding together. Americans have won the battle against material things; we have succeeded splendidly in learning how to stay alive. We must now learn to live together. Our greatest challenge is to translate the ideal of brotherhood into actuality.

There are, in our modern American society, groups of men who are constantly probing into the deeper implications of brotherhood. Each of them has discovered important work to be done, and each has volunteered to join with others who are dedicated to that work. Their very existence is a challenge and an inspiration to their fellow men. They share the conviction that the Christian message is as pertinent today as ever it was. They know that changing times lend new insights into that message. It is their job to live the completely Christian life in the light of these insights and thereby testify to its relevance. They call themselves brothers.

Most of these religious families are Roman Catholic. Some are Anglican (Protestant Episcopal). Throughout the years many other sects and denominations have experimented in communal organizations. There are as many specific types of brothers as there are specific needs to be met in our society. They engaged in education, social work, care of the sick, research, and the various administrative and manual operations necessary to the functioning of complex organizations.

Young Americans seem more conscious of their social responsibility than ever before. They do not hesitate to join in public demonstrations for the right causes. Some call it bearing witness with their bodies. Many of them feel so keenly the need for positive action that they join the Peace Corps and share the best of their experience with strangers in a foreign land. Still other young Americans are willing to bear witness for a lifetime as religious brothers. They are so convinced that they have something of value to impart that they make the imparting a life's work. They do not marry, they do not work for a salary, they go wherever they are sent, and do whatever task is assigned. They do not think that they are extraordinarily heroic or noble. They take themselves for granted.

As we will see, there have been organizations of brothers in all countries and in all ages, pre-dating Christianity. However, the brother's life seems particularly suited to American ideals. Typically American is a healthy respect for education, a strong streak of altruism, a willingness to volunteer. Typical, too, is the

Yankee ingenuity which qualifies a man to be a jack-of-all-trades. Some historians think these qualities came from the frontier, where a man had to be clever with his hands as well as with his brains. From the frontier, too, came that brash camaraderie which is so American. It was the spirit that pervaded the cabin-raisings of colonial times and the campfires of the more recent west.

Finally, there is a more profound strain which runs deeply through the American character. Governor Bradford of Plymouth voiced it long ago. "Thus out of small beginnings greater things have been produced by his hand that made all things out of nothing, and gives being to all things that are; and as one small candle may light a thousand; so the light here kindled hath shone unto many. . . ." Always a God-fearing people, Americans are convinced that there is something providential about the story of this land of ours. God meant America, so they say, to be a place where men can be free to grow to their full stature. They can be ten feet tall, not only in body but in spirit. They can pursue happiness in a bountiful land, under their own government. God had a mission for America, they say, and that mission is to provide the place on earth where men can achieve his dignity and work out his salvation.

And in all that has just been said about American characteristics and beliefs, we have been describing the reasons why young Americans today enter religious life. Brothers are living testimony to the fact that voluntarism and altruism are not dead. Many of them become educators because they think that in no other calling can they reach young people and tell them the things that matter. Many of them become mechanics or farmers or cooks, because each order needs such workers if it is to achieve its purpose. The brothers want that purpose to be achieved, they love God and know of no greater offering than their work, which they also love.

In this age when men are becoming increasingly aware of their social responsibilities, the life of a brother is more pertinent than ever. It is important to understand the brother's calling, if for no other reason than to dispel the mystery which has at times caused mistrust and suspicion. Understanding will lead to closer co-operation between brothers and laymen. Understanding will also engender admiration, leading some young men to join the ranks of the long black line of men called brothers.

This book is written for those who do not know much about the brother's life, but are sufficiently curious to have read this far.

At the outset, I must confess to an indulgence in an author's license. I have brazenly drawn upon my own order, the Marists, for examples of various sorts and I have undoubtedly slighted some very fine orders by limited references to them. However, all orders of brothers are listed in the Appendix and specific information on each will be gladly furnished to any interested inquirer. Secondly, I have shamefully ignored the magnificent work of those dedicated women of the Church, the nuns. My only excuse is that to mention them as they deserve would require another volume of this size, and that the publishers of the Careers in Depth series, wise men that they are, have arranged for just such a companion piece entitled *Your Calling as a Nun*.

YOUR CALLING AS A BROTHER

CHAPTER I

Monastic Brothers: From the Solitaries to the Mendicants

Most brothers wear a peculiar garb. They do so not because they want to appear outlandish, but because they want to remind people of their dedication to a set of values different from those of men who wear gray flannel suits and from those who wear motorcycle jackets and blue-jeans. For better or for worse, a man's code of life is judged by his apparel.

So brothers wear a peculiar garb. They did not concoct these habits (as they are called) upon the spur of the moment. Each type of dress tells the historical legacy of its wearer. It is a link with the past. A convention of religious resembles an historical tableau. The Franciscan in his brown robes and sandals might have stepped out of fourteenth-century Italy; the Christian Brother's collar is reminiscent of the lace ruff of seventeenth century French society. We need to take a backward glance through the centuries if we are to properly understand why the brothers dress as they do, and especially if we are to understand why they behave as they do.

Christ really started it. There were groups of men living in the deserts before Christ, and there are today monks who claim other founders, such as Buddha. Within the perspective of Western civilization however, Christ started it. When a young man mentioned that he had done a good job of keeping the commandments and wondered what more he might do, Christ suggested that he dispose of his property. "Come, follow Me," he said. The young man in question decided not to, but others accepted the invitation. At another time, Christ said that, while marriage was the state of life for most men, for those who could take it the unmarried state was preferable. The summons to a life of poverty and chastity were invitations or "counsels" and not commandments by any means. All men were enjoined to love both God and their neighbor, and were even told to become perfect. Still, only those to whom Christ addressed a special call were to practice poverty and chastity.

The calling of a brother is simply Christ's ever-echoing invitation to "Come, follow Me." Throughout history men have followed Him, now stressing one aspect of his life, now another. And some of these men, like other Christs, have drawn followers.

During the first three centuries Christians struggled for a place in a hostile world. In the best of times they were faced by the bad example of pagan society, and in the worst of times they were hounded down into catacombs and out into deserts. The deserts of Egypt were particularly inviting to the most venturesome among them. They went out into the desert to practice self-discipline. They were intoxicated by the message of Christ, and they scorned compromise. Some think that the first monk was Frontonius who led seventy followers into the desert of Nitria. This happened somewhere in the middle of the second century. But the most celebrated of the desert saints was Anthony whose virtue was so well known that a great number of disciples crowded around in imitation. We might call him the father of monasticism, if the monks who gathered about, each in his own cell or cave, could be thought of as forming a monastery.

It is fashionable today to regard these hermits of old with a certain disdain. Moderns are repelled by the severity of their penances and amused by the accounts of their struggles against the devil and temptation. The most severe indictment of the solitaries is that they were selfish, that they cared little or nothing about their fellow men, thinking only of saving their own souls. This attitude results from applying our own frame of reference to radically different situations. In the first place, Christians did care about their fellow men and desperately tried to spread the Good News of Christ. Their mutual charity became a byword, "See how they love one another." It would have done precious little good for them to have tried to practice modern benefactions, opening schools and hospitals, for example. They practiced social responsibility by dying as martyrs and by fleeing into deserts. Thus they bore witness with their bodies and shocked a decadent world into a new awakening.

The theme of this story is that in every age there have been people who have responded to the needs of their society. Among them were men called brothers, and the monks of the desert were the first brothers. Their rule was given them by a monk named Pachomius who became the superior of several monasteries. In the middle of the fourth century St. Basil of Caesarea established a new rule which regulated the details of the lives of those who adopted it. It called for long hours of manual work and prayer, imposing severe penances for the slightest faults. Though strict, St. Basil of Caesarea's rule was more moderate than that practiced by some of the desert hermits. Significantly, the rule of St. Basil permitted the monks to undertake the education of children. Usually this was strictly religious instruction because the early Christians thought that Christ's second coming was imminent and secular learning was a waste of time. St. Basil wrote an essay entitled *On the Reading of the Profane Authors* as a guide for his monks and other Christians. During his day Christians sent their children to pagan schools and St. Basil's essay was typical of the suspicion with which these schools were regarded.

More and more Christians found their way into the Roman classical schools as teachers. The first important Christian educator was Clement of Alexandria who died in the year 215. He saw positive value in the Latin and Greek classics and understood how they complemented the teaching of Christ. He aimed at a synthesis of knowledge and faith. If Clement had founded an order of teachers, the teaching brotherhoods of today might claim him as their founder. However, he did not, so he is simply the first of those hardy intellectual pioneers who were not afraid to risk contamination in pursuit of truth wherever it might be found.

The Emperor Julian, in 362, became concerned about the large number of Christian teachers in the schools. The ancient Roman religion was being undermined. He decreed that all teachers would have to be approved by the state; religious orthodoxy was one of the requirements. As a result the Christians founded their own schools.

The Rule of St. Basil was not very popular in the West. Most of the monks of Italy and Gaul preferred to live alone. During the fifth and sixth centuries, with the advance of the barbarians, Roman society began to break up. More and more Christians took to the countryside. Some were seeking perfection, others were seeking security. Monastery organization was rather chaotic, depending as it did on the whim of the elected superior or abbot. In 451, the Council of Chalcedon placed all monasteries under the jurisdiction of the local bishops.

St. Benedict was one of those who attracted followers to his retreat at Subiaco, much as Anthony of Egypt had drawn men into the desert before him. There was considerable difficulty between Benedict and the bishop of the place and so he withdrew to Monte Cassino. There, in 529, he founded the monastery which has lasted until today. (Actually it has been destroyed twenty times in successive wars but the monks keep rebuilding it.) Benedict is most famous because of the rule he drew up. It differed from St. Basil's in its affectionate sympathy for human weakness. His intention, as he states in the prologue to the rule, is "to establish a school of the Lord's service, in the setting forth of which we hope to order nothing that is harsh or vigorous."

In that precarious age the monasteries became islands of stability. The monks vowed to remain in the one place. They were bound to do manual work for six hours a day. Economic self-sufficiency was necessary to support not only themselves, but also any person who sought their hospitality. Though it is easy to exaggerate their importance, we might regard the monasteries as props for a tottering society when governments waned in power and cities were depopulated.

When people are mainly concerned with survival there is not much time for the finer things. Nevertheless the monks preserved learning. They had to be able to read if they were to fulfill Benedict's injunction to spend four hours a day in study. They taught the children who were brought to the monasteries for safekeeping. The monasteries were not only model farms, they also became model schools.

Of course there was the problem of what to teach, and the old question of the place of profane knowledge. Early in the fifth century Martianus Capella wrote a little book called *The Marriage of Philology and Mercury*. Presumably Philology was the fairest of all the arts. At the wedding Mercury presents his chosen bride with seven maidservants. The seven maids are the seven liberal arts; grammar, rhetoric, dialectic, arithmetic, geometry, astronomy and music. Thus the modern curriculum of arts and sciences had its genesis, although it is safe to bet that the vast majority of teachers in our liberal arts colleges never heard of *The Marriage of Philology and Mercury* or of Martianus Capella.

Boethius, a contemporary of Benedict, did more than Martianus. In his famous *Consolations of Philosophy* Boethius placed the content of pagan philosophy within a Christian context. He provided the necessary bridge between Christianity and the classics, and his Consolations became the textbook of the Middle Ages. We might say that Benedict supplied the organization and Boethius the content and direction for monastic education.

The monks could now with a clear conscience carefully copy the classics and preserve Western civilization during the period of the barbarization of Europe.

The wisdom and flexibility of the Rule of St. Benedict is illustrated by its continuance for fourteen centuries and present influence on modern society. In the United States today, most abbeys are engaged in education. However, Benedictines continue to establish their abbeys in rural areas and work at farming as well, much as they did when the whole world looked to them for guidance.

And so monasticism became one of the dominant institutions of the early Middle Ages, while the Moslem conquest was causing Europe to turn in on itself. Trade slowed to a standstill and centralized government disappeared.

Some of the monasteries were too successful, and grew wealthy and lax. Periodic reforms were thus necessary. During the eleventh century, the Carthusians were established by St. Bruno and given a rule which reminds one of the severity of Pachomius and Basil. The rule served its purpose admirably since the Carthusian Order has needed no reform since. The Carthusian even today lives a life of solitude and contemplation, joining his fellow monks only for Mass and parts of the Divine Office. He eats alone, never tastes meat and, during Lent and Advent, refrains from all types of dairy products. Yet Carthusians are remarkably healthy and long-lived. The Carthusians came to America in 1951 when they opened a monastery near Whitingham, Vermont.

The Cistercians represented another reform in the eleventh century. They attempted to return to the primitive spirit of the Benedictine rule by setting up their monasteries in the wilderness. They drained swamps and irrigated deserts. They were the pioneers of their day and led the way as a resurgent Europe moved eastward into Germany, closing its last frontiers.

St. Bernard, though not the first Cistercian, was by far the most famous. The intimate connection between monasticism and feudal society is illustrated by the fact that Bernard "retired" to a monastery and became the dominant force in Christendom.

The Cistercian Order was, in its turn, reformed in the seventeenth century by Abbot de Rance of La Grande Trappe Abbey in southern France. His followers are called Trappists, or Cistercians of the Strict Observance. Although they have been in America since 1848, their greatest growth has occurred since World War II. There were three Trappist monasteries in 1944, today there are ten. The Trappist life rivals the Carthusian in the demands it makes on human nature. The monk's seventeen hour day begins at 2:00 A.M. He spends about seven hours in prayer and about five in manual labor. The brothers spend more time in manual labor than do the choir monks. Trappists never taste meat, eggs, or fish; part of the year they go without milk and cheese. Furthermore, they communicate with each other when necessary by signs rather than by speech. Thomas Merton, a Trappist of Gethsemani Abbey in Kentucky, has done much to acquaint Americans with the Trappist way of life.

Other forces were at work in the twelfth century. Trade was increasing and breathing life into cities. The Holy Land fell to the Saracens and all Christendom stirred to the Pope's call to arms. Monasticism was one institution of that age, chivalry was another. The crusades offered the knights a chance to display their prowess for a noble cause. Off they went to the Holy Land to the sound of trumpets and on a wave of emotion.

They failed, of course, to rid the holy places of the infidel. But they succeeded in other ways. For one thing, the Italian cities became wealthy, and trade spread to the cities of the Atlantic and northern Germany. Feudalism waned and nation states began to take shape. As society changed, adaptation was necessary in the traditional monastic institutions. New orders sprang up in response to new needs. There were the Templars, the Teutonic Knights, and the Knights of Malta, for example. The notion of joining the religious life in order to fight seems almost a caricature, but these men were following the same principle as those of other ages. They employed their talents in the best interests of God and society, as they saw these interests. Actually, there was more the idea of defending the holy places than of attacking Moslems. Except as honorary societies, these military orders did not outlast the age of chivalry. Because the Moslem enemy found a lucrative business in capturing Christians and holding them for ransom, orders were founded to raise money for their rescue. One such, the Trinitarians, by adapting to other works of mercy, has lasted until today.

Another problem was that contact with Moslem culture had introduced disturbing intellectual currents. Educated Europeans were not sure that Aristotle, as interpreted by Islamic scholars like Averroes, could be reconciled with traditional Christian philosophy as interpreted by Boethius. Equally disturbing was the effect of wealth on society. Westerners became fascinated with the luxuries of the East, and Gospel simplicity was forgotten, even by many of the clergy.

The response to these two problems was the formation of the great *mendicant* orders founded by two very famous contemporaries, Dominic and Francis of Assisi. Dominic's first followers were sent to preach in that part of southern France where the Albigensians had adopted unorthodox doctrines. Dominic was vexed to find that the pomp of the priests of the region was exceeded only by their ignorance of the doctrine they were upholding. His monks were to be itinerant preachers. Forbidden to own land, they were to live principally on alms. Certainly, here was a revolutionary moment in the history of monasticism. Benedict had attempted to stabilize monks in rural settings and now Dominic was setting them loose in cities. They became especially influential in the great university centers of Bologna and Paris. As Dominican houses spread, the founder gave them an admirable form of organization combining the essential features of checks and balances, federalism and democracy. The rule says not a word about manual labor, every spare moment was to go into the intellectual training necessary to the pursuit of truth. The Dominicans gave new direction to European higher education. Philosophy was ranked above the liberal arts, but just below theology.

From that day to this, Dominicans have occupied an important place in higher education. Since this is a book about brothers, one might ask what part they play in the Dominican Order. It is true that the preachers are priests, but they are freed to preach and study by the lay brothers who do the manual chores necessary to every successful operation.

If Dominic's strength lay in his intellect, Francis' was in his affections. He did not endeavor so much to know God as to love Him. And such a delightful person was Francis that everyone loved him, from Pope Innocent III to the Sultan of Egypt. In fact, every living thing loved him, including fish, fowl and various kinds of animals, the most celebrated of which was the wolf of Gubbio. Francis was one of those rare sensitive souls who emerge from time to time and who are able to sense how present God is in all creation. Calling the sun his brother and the moon his sister, his life was one long poem. Francis' forte was not in doing, but in being. His example drew followers, and he was not quite sure what he should do with them. He was not even sure of his own vocation. At times he thought he should be doing something useful, like converting the infidels. At other times he considered abandoning his brethren in order to live as a solitary. The one thing he was sure of, that the brothers should observe absolute poverty, turned out to be impossible in practice.

The question was so vexing that it resulted in a schism within the Order. Three of today's Franciscans claim the Poor Man of Assisi as founder. The Conventuals, Friars Minor or Observants, and the Capuchins. Several American orders follow the rule which Francis drew up originally for pious laymen: the Franciscan Friars of the Atonement (Graymoor), the Brothers of the Regular Third Order of St. Francis (Franciscan Brothers of Brooklyn), the Third Order Regular of St. Francis of Penance (Franciscan Fathers), the Brothers of the Poor of St. Francis, the Franciscan Missionary Brothers, and the Franciscan Brothers of the Holy Cross.

In addition, there is a Protestant Franciscan branch, the Order of the Poor Brethren of St. Francis, located at Little Portion Monastery, Mount Sinai, Long Island, New York. Here, there are as many brothers as priests, and no distinction is made between them except that the priests administer the sacraments. All do manual work, all give retreats and missions. All have a seat, voice, and vote in Community Meetings and all can hold office. In this equalization of the traditional classes, the Protestant Franciscans have anticipated their Roman brethren.

The sudden appearance on the scene of the mendicant orders and their astonishing success in captivating Christians of all stations brought with it some of the same side-effects that have accompanied other reform movements. In the first place, the monks of the ancient orders were offended—because, by implicit and even explicit statement, it was they who needed reformation. They had lost touch with the deeper needs of their day. As the mendicants attracted more vocations, the older orders drew fewer. Bishops and parish priests regarded the activity of the mendicants as an intrusion. From that day to this, the pastors are supreme in their parishes. They disliked the way their flocks deserted them in preference to the mendicants. The professors in the universities resented the obvious popularity of the Dominicans and Franciscans.

Imitators sprang up in all countries. More and more pious laymen began to organize new confraternities and to ask for papal recognition. At such times, the Church has demonstrated that although it is in favor of zeal it is against inefficiency. At the Council of Lyons, in 1274, it put a stop to the formation of new mendicant orders just as some centuries before it had put a stop to the proliferation of monasteries. Other than the Dominicans and Franciscans, only the Carmelites and Augustinians were permitted to continue in existence as mendicant orders. The Servites might also be included in this group.

The Carmelites offer a good example of radical adaptation. A group of hermits, originally settled in Palestine and tracing their beginnings to Elias the Prophet, they had obtained a rule in 1207 which bound them to a life of mortification, prayer and solitude. When they transferred their order to Europe, in 1247, they were given mendicant status by the Pope and abandoned their hermitages for convents in the towns. They began to devote themselves to study and preaching to such good effect that, by the end of the century, hardly a trace remained of their earlier form of life.

The fourth mendicant order were the Hermits of St. Augustine, originally groups of monks who went about Italy begging and preaching in the manner of the Franciscans. Under papal direction they went through successive steps toward centralization until, by 1356, they formed a single congregation under one superior.

By the beginning of the fourteenth century there were 80,000 friars in the mendicant orders. The most numerous were the Franciscans with 35,000. Compared to the total population of Europe the membership in the mendicant orders was astonishingly high, higher in fact than the world total in the same orders today. The mendicants offered an expression for the great spiritual foment at the dawn of the Renaissance.

CHAPTER II

Teaching Brothers: From the Brothers of the Common Life to the Brothers of the Christian Schools

The same foment which produced the mendicants caused an upsurge in the number of schools. Bishops had always conducted schools at their cathedrals for aspirants to the priesthood. After the year 1200, the schools became better organized and more numerous. They replaced monasteries as centers of Christian culture. The smaller schools taught the so-called trivium: grammar, rhetoric, and dialectic. The larger cathedral schools offered the quadrivium also, adding thus arithmetic, geometry, music, and astronomy. There were not enough cathedral schools to satisfy the demands of the growing towns, so municipal schools were established by the town councils, modeled upon the cathedral schools and always with the approval of the bishop or his chancellor.

As great teachers began to appear in the cathedral and town schools, crowds of pupils flocked about them. The intellectual quickening was sparked as Arabic scholars introduced Greek mathematical, medical, and philosophical works. The direction taken by higher education is known as scholasticism. In general, it was a means and a method of employing *reason* in a search for truth. Reason was exalted as it had not been since the advent of Christianity. This intellectual current attracted the energies of the mendicants, especially the Dominicans. St. Albert the Great and St. Thomas Aquinas were among the foremost scholastic teachers. St. Thomas' masterpiece, the *Summa Theologica,* was quite radical for his day, relying heavily as it did upon the authority of Aristotle. It was soon accepted as orthodox thinking by Christian philosophers. The successes of the mendicants led to an inevitable decline. Gifts were showered on them, land was donated to them. A series of disasters—the Black Death, the Hundred Years War, the Great Schism in the Western Church—all hastened the demoralization of society and the weakening of religion's influence.

Reforms were tried, but they were not well directed. For example, restraints were imposed on the intellectual life of the Dominicans, and what had been their glory was now considered a distraction. Understandably, the desired renewal was not achieved. The Carmelites alone succeeded, to an extent, in returning to their earlier tradition of contemplation and austerity.

During the late fourteenth century a new interest in classical learning began to capture men's minds. Scholasticism had become too abstract, too other-worldly. The new emphasis was the study of man and of those things which contributed to the enjoyment of his life. The movement was called humanism; the cultural awakening which accompanied it was the Renaissance.

At this juncture appeared a group of educators of especial interest for our purposes. The fourteenth century was like our own in that religion was in retreat, and material interests were assuming greater importance. The Brothers of the Common Life were organized to adapt the Christian message to the needs of the times. Expert in theology, they had also to become expert in the new learning. Gerhard Groot, who founded the new association, was convinced that education was the best way to inaugurate a reform among his contemporaries. Groot regarded monastic life as the most perfect, but his brotherhood was to provide a modified monasticism for lay people who wanted to live a better life than they could in a distracted society. Their prime concern was the religious education of young people. The brotherhood included some priests who served as chaplains. Constant industry was necessary, since the brothers had to support themselves by whatever skills they knew in addition to their work as teachers. Their zeal contrasted favorably with the mendicants recent tendency to a life of idleness and begging. Just as the older orders had resented the activities of the mendicant friars, so now the friars obstructed the new form of religious life. At the Council of Constance, a Dominican named Grabow accused the Brothers of the Common Life of living in sin—since it was a sin, he maintained, to live in common without the vows of poverty, chastity, and obedience. The brothers were defended by the celebrated scholar Gerson, and were upheld by the decision of the Council.

The brothers did not found schools of their own. Instead, they opened boarding houses near existing schools and offered supplementary religious education. In some cases the brothers were invited to take over the administration of municipal schools. In these respects the Brothers of the Common Life might be considered very modern. Some of today's teaching brothers feel that they should open similar houses of study on secular campuses, and that they should enter the public system of education. Also modern was the brothers' insistence on the importance of Scripture study in the vernacular as a means of fostering solid piety among the laity. It is safe to say, to their lasting credit, that no other group of educators in the Catholic Church laid such stress on the role of Scripture study until the renewal of the present century.

The pupils of the Brothers of the Common Life were more famous than the brothers themselves. Some of them were Alexander Heguis, Rudolph Agricola, Jacob Wimpheling. More important was Thomas a Kempis, who became an Augustinian monk and the author of the *Imitation of Christ,* and those two giants of Christian humanism, Erasmus and Vives. Through these men, the brothers have exerted a lasting influence on the development of modern education, especially in the study of classic literature and vernacular languages.

With the Reformation in the sixteenth century the brothers' houses came under the control of either the Jesuits or Protestant teachers. A few lasted until the time of Napoleon when they were suppressed.

The quiet work of the good brothers, though more effective than that of the older orders in reclaiming Christians to a life of piety, did not stem the general decline of the Church. That rude shock was delivered by another student of the brothers who had become an Augustinian monk—Martin Luther. The great defection from the Catholic Church which Luther initiated caused a trauma within the Church, the Counter Reformation.

During the massive readjustment of the sixteenth century, the Capuchins emerged as the reform element among the Franciscans, the Discalced Carmelites were the followers of St. Theresa of Avila and St. John of the Cross. However, the great innovation of the sixteenth century were the new orders of priests, living in community and pledged to poverty, but prepared to undertake any and every form of apostolic work in the world. In most cases, these orders admitted brothers who did the manual and administrative chores for the priests. The Oratorian Fathers, now established in the United States, are one such order. The Piarists, or Clerks Regular of the Religious Schools, have also found their way through the years to modern America. Another society, this one confined to brothers, were the Hospitallers of St. John of God. Their hospital work is as valuable in modern Boston and Los Angeles as it was in their founder's Granada.

But by far and away the most influential order of the sixteenth century and, in fact, since then, were the Jesuits. Well educated, well organized, they vowed obedience to the Pope and became supranational in an age of increasing nationalism. They became the shock troops of the Church, fighting on all fronts, preaching and teaching, advising popes and princes. With Peter Canisius they won back parts of the Rhine and the Danube Valleys for Catholicism. Their rivalry with the favored Dominicans kept them out of Spanish lands, but they were welcomed by Portugal instead. With Francis Xavier they preached the faith in India and in Japan. They established model plantations in Brazil called "reductions." They arrived with the French in Canada and wrote a remarkable story of courage and dedication in the annals of North American history.

In the progress of our history of brothers, the Reformation intrudes a discordant note. Just as the Brothers of the Common Life seemed to be on the verge of identifying dedicated laymen with the business of education, the Jesuits replaced them as the schoolmasters of Catholic Europe. There were, and still are, brothers among the Jesuits, but only in our time have they begun to take a place beside the priests as professional educators. The great service which the Jesuits did for modern teaching orders of priests and brothers was to set a standard of excellence. Each Jesuit was taught to be a dedicated teacher by dedicated teachers. In all, the training took then, and still takes, a total of fourteen years. Teaching became thus a way of life rather than a necessary interruption of pastoral activity. Their *ratio studiorum* provided a uniform plan for all their schools; students were graded for achievement; the curriculum was adapted to varying ages and abilities. There were no fees for tuition. Their classes were small and selective; they deliberately sought out the better students as potential leaders of society.

The Reformation produced a number of Protestant sects, some of which engaged in the work of education. The most significant, because John Amos Comenius was associated with it, was a Bohemian religious society called Unity of Brethren. Comenius was a Renaissance man himself, a pansophic genius, who visualized education as the instrument for the redemption of mankind. Schools, he argued, must be made available to all; learning must be both practical and pleasant. He outlined a series of schools, each lasting six years. Perhaps his greatest contribution was his theory of standardized teaching based on large classes and the use of a textbook. Comenius was not able to put his ideas into effect on the scale he would have liked, but others would undertake that task. Like the Jesuits, he set a high standard for modern educators.

The German Pietists, for example, borrowed from Comenius in setting up their schools in Germany. August Hermann Francke was their foremost educator. For the Pietists, no education was so useful and realistic as religious education. Study of the New Testament occupied a principal place in the curriculum. The importance of Francke and the Pietists is that they were largely responsible for the German school system which grew up in the eighteenth century. They also had a major influence on American colonial education.

As the seventeenth century lengthened, a new social problem crystallized. There were no means of teaching the children of the growing urban artisan class, who themselves would be artisans. The Church was slow to adapt to the demands of this new middle class. Calvinism exerted a strong attraction on these people, stressing as it did the virtues of thrift and industry, promising God's blessings to the elect in this life as well as in the next. Vincent de Paul, the justly celebrated Monsieur Vincent, was one of those who plunged into the sweatshops and prisons, into the hovels and dark alleys. He founded a society of priests who devoted themselves to works of charity. Their proper name is Congregation of the Mission, but they are better known as Vincentians. Other smaller orders of priests began to pay more attention to the poor, but the great problem was that there was no adequate school system for the urban middle classes, much less for the poor. The parish schools were hopelessly inadequate. The professional lay teachers preferred to teach the wealthy since they also preferred to work for pay. The Jesuits had done an admirable job in setting up a massive operation, but they were interested in secondary education and in the better students.

In short, the situation was a peculiarly modern one. The problems of an urban proletariat were here to stay. New social institutions had to be adapted to the changed world, just as new economic and political systems had to be formulated. It was the age of mercantilism, of joint stock companies, of growing demands for representative government. The great innovator in the field of education was John Baptist de LaSalle. He thought that the task of education was essentially a layman's rather than that of a priest. He also thought that it was sufficiently noble to attract young men to work for the love of God instead of for pay. Therefore he gathered interested young men around him and taught them to be teachers. The result was the first modern teaching society of brothers, the Brothers of the Christian Schools. Theorists, Comenius for example, had advocated group instruction, and it had been tried at intervals throughout the history of education. However, it was de LaSalle who introduced simultaneous teaching to seventeenth-century France. It was also he who established the first teachers' training school. This he did for the professional education of his brothers in 1687. One of de LaSalle's more radical changes, considering the strong classic emphasis since the Renaissance, was the abandonment of Latin in favor of the vernacular. There were strong objections from the traditionalists, including those who regarded Catholic education as primarily for the purpose of recruiting priests.

LaSalle was successful beyond his expectations. His brothers became expert in the practical elementary education of boys to the life of a good Christian in the world. His system provided a model for the dozens of teaching orders which would appear in Europe during the nineteenth century.

The eighteenth century was the Enlightened Age; faith in reason and science seemed to be replacing religion. Embattled since the Reformation, the Church was increasingly on the defensive. The battlefield was man's mind and the weapons were ideas. Two new organizations specialized in this warfare. They were the Passionists, founded in 1720 by a Florentine priest St. Paul of the Cross, and the Redemptorists, begun in Naples in 1732 by St. Alphonsus Liguori. Both societies based their preaching on contemplation; both were reactions against the overstress on intellectualism.

Just at the time when the talents of the Jesuits were most needed, they were disbanded. The suppression wreaked havoc on the complex world-wide operations which that society had established, especially their school system. Success had harmed the great society, as it had the mendicants and the earlier monasticism. Jesuits had become involved in commercial ventures and in politics. Their enemies included the enlightened philosophers on one hand, and the Jansenists on the other. Moreover, they gave the impression that they were exploiting the Church rather than serving it. They were expelled from the Portuguese Empire in 1759, from France and her colonies in 1762, and from the Spanish realm in 1767. Finally, in response to relentless pressure, Clement XIV disbanded the society in 1773. The Catholic rulers of Europe made haste to enforce the papal decision. Ignoring for the emergency their traditional obedience to the Pope, the Jesuits refused to die out. On the theory that where a law is not promulgated it is not a law, they sought refuge in those countries which were hostile to papal decrees. They were welcomed by Frederick the Great of Prussia (who said he would welcome Moslems as readily), and by that other enlightened unbeliever Catherine of Russia. These benevolent despots of the eighteenth century considered it their duty to undertake measures for the popular welfare which had formerly been conducted under the auspices of the Church. Frederick the Great took the lead in setting up a compulsory attendance system in government controlled schools. He welcomed the Jesuits as professional schoolmasters. The expulsion of the Jesuits from the Catholic countries was largely due to the nationalist desire to use education to serve the ends of the state. National education in France received a powerful impetus with the Revolution in 1789.

The Jesuits were only the first of many orders to undergo suppression. Emperor Joseph II, devout Catholic though he was, banished all contemplative orders. The French Revolution was the culmination of a general movement. In 1792, monks and nuns were turned out of their convents. Some religious underwent martyrdom; most simply returned to "the world." In all those lands penetrated by the armies of the republic, religious houses were closed. Napoleon was ruthless in finishing the job of suppression. He discovered that the Jesuits had renewed their activity under the title "Fathers of the Faith," and dealt with them severely. For a while he tolerated the Christian Brothers; but finally they, too, met the same fate as the other religious orders.* In 1799, Novalis wrote, "Catholicism is almost played out. The old Papacy is laid in the tomb, and Rome for the second time has become a ruin."

* The Emperor soon discovered that there were not enough schoolmasters to replace the brothers; he allowed them to be reorganized in 1803.

CHAPTER III

Modern Orders Emerge: Nineteenth Century France Produces the New Teaching Communities

As the nineteenth century began, religious orders were in a perilous state. It was as if men's energies had been so concentrated in the effort to establish a perfect society based on reason that Christianity had become superfluous. The ardor for liberty, equality, and fraternity was quenched by the bloodbath of the Napoleonic wars. In the wake of these wars, Europe lay stricken. Religion had been forsaken and rationalism had failed; men were demoralized and disillusioned. The great reaction set in after Waterloo. Statesmen tried to restore things as they were before the Revolution. Thinkers exalted emotions and talked less of the infallibility of reason. Romantics rediscovered the genius of Christianity and the charms of the Middle Ages.

In all this, it was impossible of course to ignore the events of the last twenty-five years. The restoration resulted in an uneasy compromise between the old and the new, rather than a complete victory for the forces of reaction. It was not surprising that in such a climate a conscience-stricken France should be as extreme in restoring religious orders as she had been in getting rid of them.

The Jesuits demonstrated that the rumors of their demise had been premature by rebounding in numbers and influence. However, they continued to exhibit the same uncompromising attitudes that had got them banished in the first place, and thus they were expelled from their former refuge Russia in

1820, from Switzerland in 1848, Germany in 1872, and France in 1880. All the while, their numbers and influence continued to increase, banishments notwithstanding.

The old monastic orders revived with the renewal of interest in the Middle Ages. The Benedictine Abbey of Solesmes showed the way in a study of the liturgy of the Church, a study which has resulted in the astonishing interest in liturgical reform in the present century. The Franciscans showed new strength as missionaries. The Friars Minor were especially active in Latin America where religious orders had been banned since the independence of the new nations. The Capuchins specialized in Biblical study and laid the foundation for the second powerful force at work in the twentieth-century Church. Liturgical reform and a new interpretation of the Scriptures would make religion more comprehensible to the laity and would establish the necessary climate for the great ecumenical movement.

The Dominicans had virtually disappeared from Europe. Like the Jesuits they had taken advantage of the separation of Church and State in the United States. Slowly, they returned to a position of intellectual pre-eminence. Their most famous preacher was Lacordaire who swayed much of France from the pulpit of Notre Dame.

Back came the more recent societies: the Sulpicians, Vincentians, Redemptorists, and Passionists. Especially rapid was the renewed growth of the Christian Brothers. It was now that the example of John Baptist de LaSalle exerted a powerful influence on other priests. An entire generation had grown up under an educational system hostile to religion. The most immediate need was to reclaim the new generation. What better way could be devised than LaSalle's method of gathering dedicated religious teachers together and setting up schools? Like LaSalle, these founders were usually magnetic personalities who inspired others by their own enthusiasm.

Such a man was Edmund Ignatius Rice, a layman who devoted his wealth to the education of the poor youth of Waterford, Ireland. His first school was opened in 1804. Young men came in such numbers to join him that he was able to establish twenty-seven schools before his death in 1844. His society, the Christian Brothers of Ireland, has flourished to an even greater extent in the United States. Ireland also gave birth to a second order of teaching brothers, in 1808, when Bishop Delaney of Kildare formed the Brothers of St. Patrick. The way to America was somewhat more devious for the Patricians. They arrived in 1948, having come by way of India and Australia.

It was in postwar France that the most remarkable religious quickening occurred. Twenty religious orders of men in operation in the United States today originated in nineteenth-century France. Most of them were concerned with education and most were founded in the decade after the Restoration. Their influence today is enormous since it is exercised on an ever-expanding student population through some twenty colleges, two hundred high schools, and nearly one hundred elementary schools.

These congregations cannot be properly understood unless social conditions in restoration France are understood. Chateaubriand, the literary hero of the religious revival, wrote a description of the collapse of the Roman Empire:

> When the dust rising from the wreck of so many monuments settled down, when death silenced the groans of so many victims, when the noise from the fall of the colossus ceased, then a cross was seen, and at the foot of the cross a new world. A few priests, carrying the Gospel and seated on these ruins, raised up society amid the tombs, as Jesus Christ brought back to life the children of those who believed in Him.

The description fits post-Napoleonic France. It is especially apt because the agents of reform in both epochs were lay religious for the most part. There were simply not enough priests to do what had to be done. Their numbers had been so drastically reduced from 1800 to 1815 that the country districts were entirely without the services of priests. The dearth of knowledge was profound. When a zealous priest was assigned to any of the most neglected areas, his first impulse was to appeal to laymen for assistance. Generally, the priest would have to first teach the assistants the rudiments of knowledge. Amid the general conditions of destitution, the teachers could expect no revenue. They were bound to a life of poverty and manual labor by force of circumstances, if by nothing else. However, unless there were something more, no young man would continue to serve his pastor after he himself received a sufficient education. Besides, the law required universal military training, and many aspiring teachers were diverted from a life of dedication by their army experience. Exemption was necessary, and the only way to secure it was to obtain recognition as a religious order. In this, there was always the inspiring example of the Christian Brothers to guide other founders.

Thus the plethora of new religious orders can be explained very pragmatically. The most efficient way to reclaim an entire generation from the materialism of the Revolution was to devise a system for mass education. Clergy and politicians agreed on one major reason for educating the masses. They must be convinced not to overthrow the regime again. Education tended to be practical rather than theoretical, authoritarian rather than democratic.

We would be wrong if we omitted the reason that motivated the priests and brothers who pioneered the new congregations. That was, of course, the same that motivated the first hermits who fled into the deserts. They knew of no better way of imitating Christ in the service of their fellow men. Their opportunity was their call.

It is not surprising that the priest founders should have grounded their followers in the rather austere spirituality they had absorbed from their Sulpician teachers in the seminaries. Nor is it surprising that they would want to graft onto the infant orders the trappings of monasticism in an age which was discovering anew the glories of the Middle Ages.

Not all of the new orders survived, of course. In the first place, they met with the same coolness which established interests have exhibited toward innovators in all ages. They were opposed by certain bishops and pastors who saw them as competitors; they met with increasing regulation by the state; they were only tolerated by the Church.

The less efficient groups died out or merged with the more successful. The general movement of the orders was, in fact, affected by the currents of contemporary society. It was a period in which bold entrepreneurs with a goal and a knack for organization put together great commercial combinations. The founders of the nineteenth-century religious orders were children of their age. Invariably, they were strong personalities, leaders of men. Each stamped his institute with his own character, so that even today the influence of "the Founder" is strongly felt.

Such a personality was Marcellin Champagnat. He was the schoolmate of John Vianney, better known as the Curé of Ars, co-founder of a new missionary society, the Marist Fathers, and founder of an order of teachers, the Marist Brothers. A practical man of great physical strength and extraordinary determination, he met head-on the massive ignorance of the people of the mountain country near Lyons. As an object lesson that one man does make a difference, he recruited young men, built a house for them, taught them to earn a living in certain domestic manufactures, and sent them out to catechize the mountain hamlets. He engineered mergers with two other new orders whose spirit was compatible. More and more young men came and stayed, so that from two in 1817, the number of Marists grew to two hundred and eighty by 1840, the year of Champagnat's death. Five years later, the total had surpassed six hundred. Meanwhile, the Marist Fathers were expanding at a healthy rate. Father Colin, their superior, thought it best that the two Marist orders be independent of each other, and so it has been since that time. A golden moment which reunited the two orders was the impressive ceremony in St. Peter's, in the year 1955, when Pope Pius XII proclaimed Champagnat Blessed. This is the step which precedes canonization, the declaration of sainthood, the Church's highest accolade.

Another contemporary of Colin and Champagnat, and a Marist for a time, became a founder and was later beatified (given the title Blessed). This was Julian Eymard, whose congregation was primarily for the propagation of devotion to the Holy Eucharist. Among these Blessed Sacrament Fathers, brothers serve as sacristans, clerks, and skilled technicians.

To continue linking the new orders, Champagnat dedicated his new order at the shrine of Fourvieve in Lyons. Another man, Andrew Coindre, founded the same kind of society at the same time and in the same place. His brothers were a teaching order and bore the name Brothers of the Sacred Heart. Like the Marists, this new order mushroomed. All the new societies considered missionary work a prime responsibility and thus all have spread throughout the world in what seems an inordinately short time. The growth and direction of each society has depended to a great extent on the location of the first missions. The Sacred Heart Brothers began their missionary effort in Mobile, Alabama, in 1847. Since then they have been especially numerous in the South.

Another coincidence was that in the year Champagnat founded a teaching order bearing the name of Mary, so did another priest. Their names are even similar. Father William Joseph Chaminade founded the Society of Mary, in Bordeaux, in 1817. They are called Marianists and are fated to be forever confused with Marists, and vice versa, a situation which both orders have long since become accustomed to and, in fact, really don't mind.

An unusual feature of Chaminade's order was a deliberate intermingling of priests and brothers. Conscious of the fact that democracy was a permanent effect of the Revolution, Chaminade incorporated the principle into his Society of Mary. Some of the brothers are ordained in order to act as chaplains in the various houses, but all are on an equal footing. The superior may be either priest or brother. Also unusual was his decision that the brothers should not wear any distinctive garb. They would dress like other laymen; today they wear black suits and ties. Their priests dress like other priests. Uniquely, Marianists wear a gold ring to signify their fidelity to their vows.

Father Chaminade might have been speaking for all the new orders when he sent his emissary to secure recognition from the Minister of Instruction. "Make it clear to him that France is lost if we do not save the coming generation. The parents do not teach their children—and in default of them, who is to do it? *

The Marianists soon opened schools in Alsace. Therefore, when Bishop Purcell sought German-speaking teachers for the

* Interestingly, New York's Bishop Hughes made a similar comment a few years later. In 1843, he asked the Jesuits to set up a school in New York. "Unless something be done in time to multiply a priesthood and provide Catholic education for the youth, thousands of souls must perish for want of the bread of life. This is the critical period for the Church in America, this is the important period for laying the foundations in every kind of religious establishment which will grow until the growth of this young American Empire is achieved."

immigrants who settled in Cincinnatti, he approached these Alsatian Marianists. In 1849, Father Leon Meyer made the great crossing with four brothers. In 1850, they opened St. Mary's Institute in Dayton, Ohio. As the Sacred Heart Brothers spread from the South, so the Marianists based themselves in the Mid-West.

Of the new teaching societies, the first one to reach the United States was founded later than the others. Basil Anthony Moreau was as missionary-minded as were the others, but he was a shade more energetic. At any rate, only six years after he founded the Congregation of the Holy Cross at Le Mans, France, seven members arrived in the United States. This was September 13, 1841; the leader of the mission group was Father Edward Sorin, with him were six brothers. They went directly to Vincennes, Indiana, to report to Bishop Hailandiere who had asked them to come to this country. In February of the next year they began a new school, which is described thusly in the Catholic Directory of 1845:

> This institution—under the patronage of the Right Rev. Bishop of Vincennes, and directed by the Rev. E. Sorin—is open for the reception of young men of any religious profession, without preference or distinction. The location is on an eminence, and is one of the most healthy in the state, situated six miles from the town of Washington, Indiana.

The location has become better known as South Bend, and the school has grown into the most famous Catholic institution in the United States, Notre Dame. It seems fitting that the first venture of a teaching brotherhood in the United States should have maintained its prominence. The Directory of 1845 calls the congregation the Brothers of St. Joseph; the name distinguished them from the priests with whom they were associated in the Congregation of the Holy Cross. There was always a tendency toward a separation of the priests and brothers which was not formally recognized until 1945 when the brothers and priests were separated into different provinces. The priests of the order continue to staff Notre Dame.

It is interesting to note that while the Marist Brothers and Fathers formed two separate orders from the beginning, and the Marianists have been united from the beginning, the Holy Cross Congregation has tried both systems.

The Viatorians are another of the family of teaching orders from the south of France. Priests and brothers live in community; they have preserved a tradition of learning and scholarship implanted by their founder Louis Querbes, a priest of Lyons, France. The biography of Father Champagnat recounts how the Archbishop of Lyons urged him to affiliate his Marist Brothers with the Clerics of St. Viator. Father Champagnat resisted manfully and successfully, citing "an entirely different spirit" as his reason. Doubtlessly, he was right, since although to an outside observer the orders seem alike, each carefully preserved its own emphases and traditions. The Viatorians have specialized in higher education, for instance, whereas the Marists have concentrated on primary and, later, secondary education, with a special concern for the less well-to-do.

Two other teaching orders have the same name and shared the same founder, but are separate. Abbé Gabriel Deshayes, in 1819, together with Abbé Jean de La Mennais, founded the Brothers of Christian Instruction of Ploermel, who quickly spread to the French Antilles, Haiti, and Canada. In 1903, they opened a school in Plattsburg, New York. Soon afterwards, Deshayes revived Grignon de Montfort's foundations in the Vendée, which were on the point of extinction. They were also called Brothers of Christian Instruction, of St. Gabriel, in honor of the abbé's patron saint. Only recently have the Brothers of St. Gabriel reached the United States, by way of Canada.

Belgium contributed two teaching brotherhoods which have located in the United States. The Brothers of Charity were founded by Canon Peter Triest of Ghent and have devoted their services to the more difficult kinds of educational work, the deaf, dumb, and blind, the mentally unstable, and juvenile offenders. The second Belgian foundation was consciously oriented toward the United States. Theodore James Ryken was one of the numerous European visitors to Jacksonian America who dedicated themselves to the improvement of the young democracy. Ryken returned to his native Holland, determined to found a society of brothers who would teach in the new parochial schools which the Catholic bishops were setting up at the time. He interested enough young men to open a school in Belgium, in 1839. His dream was realized in 1854 when Bishop Spaulding invited his brothers to Kentucky. Ryken had adopted a new name in religion, Brother Francis Xavier and his order became the Brothers of St. Francis Xavier, or Xaverians.

The sudden appearance of all these new teaching societies, and we have not mentioned the new organizations of religious women, presented those ecclesiastical dignitaries who are concerned with rules and regulations with something of a dilemma. Before the appearance of the Jesuits all of the older orders took solemn vows of poverty, chastity, and obedience. St. Ignatius had his Jesuits take temporary vows before their final profession of solemn vows. After forty years of debate, Rome ruled that these Jesuits were also to be considered religious. However, they were exceptions to the general rule that only those who took solemn vows were religious. Rome was clearly reluctant to guarantee a new form of life which was not patterned after the older monastic orders. The ten congregations of brothers which were approved between 1820 and 1825 were defined as "charitable organizations" with no recognition of vows. The authorities would have preferred another term, promises or engagements, for example.

One horn of the dilemma was that the French government, in its Restoration collaboration with the Church, would recognize only those religious orders which Rome recognized. If no recognition was forthcoming, then the entire newly erected educational structure would be secularized once more. The new orders were not allowed to proffer solemn vows; simple vows which accomplished the same purposes were the rule. Pope Pius IX finally, in 1857, made simple vows obligatory for all male religious in the new institutes. The decision was significant. The Church had become convinced that men could lead a holy life within a modern congregation as well as they could under the older monastic forms; moreover, it was a healthy and rewarding life even in purely human values and therefore worthy of official endorsement.

CHAPTER IV

The Secular Institutes: A New Form of Religious Life Among the Old

The new orders of lay religious were actually a compromise between traditional religious life and a life of perfection within secular life. The private, almost clandestine, aspect of some of the more radical new societies was another effect of the French Revolution. The Jesuit Father, Pierre de Cloriviere, made his final vows just five days before his society was suppressed in 1773. He continued his work, as did many of his confreres, but as a secular and with a degree of furtiveness. During the Revolution he organized two societies, one for priests and one for women. They had no distinctive garb, nor did they live in common in a convent. His two organizations were the forerunners of the newest movement in the Church, the Secular Institutes. Although the society for priests, that of the Sacred Heart, was allowed to die out during the nineteenth century, it was revived in 1919. The other one, for women, still exists under the name Daughters of Mary.

Other similar groups of priests and laymen continued to appear during the century. They wore no distinguishing clothing; they had little or no community life, and yet they took the three vows of religion. As we have indicated, the Church recognized the religious institutes which conferred simple vows in 1857. Nothing was said about the new secular institutes. In 1889, a new decree allowed the approval of institutes of women in which some members lived in common and others at home, with vows but without habits. But it was made explicit that approval did not make such associations "religious." Their vows were neither solemn nor simple. Rather they were "private." The failure to achieve complete approval did not stem the movement in the least. Members of the secular institutes were quite content to have their organizations referred to as "associations of the faithful." Thus it was that the new Code of Canon Law, formulated at the turn of the century, imposed a greater degree of uniformity among the religious institutes such as the teaching brotherhoods, but passed over in deliberate silence any mention of the secular institutes.

Charles de Foucauld is the twentieth-century inspiration for the secular brotherhoods. His life was an adventure story which is almost incredible. He was a twentieth-century Anthony returning to the desert to find Christ. He first became interested in the desert when, as an army private, he was sent to live among the Moslems of Morocco. His brilliant book about this experience, *Reconnaissance in Morocco,* made him famous. Something deeply bothered de Foucauld and he retired to a Trappist monastery in the Alps to think about it. He then moved to a poorer monastery in French Syria and encountered Moslems again. He began to work for them, living among them. Finally, he realized what he had to do. He had to serve Christ in the unserved poor, and he had to bring Christ to them in his own person.

He returned to Paris and drew up a rule for a new religious order, the Little Brothers of Jesus. The first rule was that every brother live and work exclusively among the poorest of men, who were Christ's brothers. Charles set the example; he went to the Moroccan village of Beni-Abbes. For three years he was ignored, and no followers joined him. He moved his hut a thousand miles deeper into the Sahara to Tomarrair. In December, 1916, he was dragged from his hut by a savage tribe of raiders and was shot.

Charles de Foucauld had introduced a new emphasis, if not a new concept, into religious life. It is the idea that it is a noble thing simply to be present among the most downtrodden of the earth, not so much to convert them, or to uplift them, not at all to westernize them or even to alleviate their condition. There was nothing of the "White Man's Burden" condescension about de Foucauld. There was not even the energetic educational activity of the Peace Corps. He shared the lot of the poor and he loved them because Christ was among them. He died without the satisfaction of attracting even a single follower. But after his death his order grew gradually. Brother René Voillaume refounded the order in southern Oran, in 1934; today the Little Brothers of Jesus number over two hundred. During the day they work as laborers in the factories or on the farms. When night comes they meet by threes and fours for prayers and discussions, as well as for the mutual encouragement community life affords. Rome's disapproval of the worker-priest movement was not extended to the worker-brother movement. The brothers go where priests would not be welcome.

As the movement spread, Father Augustine Gemelle, a Franciscan, did more than anyone else to promote its cause. He brought the various groups together and became their advocate before Pope Pius XI. He himself describes the first congress of secular institutes.

> In 1938, on May 20th, was held at St. Gall in the Episcopal Curia an assembly little known but important in the religious history of the Church. Twenty delegates of ten different nationalities presented in common their aspirations and experiences for a new kind of life consecrated to God. In these

countries the movements had been created at the same time without one having any knowledge of the other—with what astonishment were they able to discover the identity of their views and their organizations.

It was clear that the secular institutes were following the same well-worn path which each group of religious innovators had trod before them. There is, first, the pioneer period during which daring radicals experiment with new solutions to basically old problems; secondly, the longer period of probation during which Christians actually try to live the new form of life under the critical eye of Churchmen and members of established institutions; thirdly, there is the period of acceptance when theologians and canon lawyers discover that the new organizations can be fit into the general structure; and, finally, there is official approval, usually expressed by a papal decree. The secular institutes met this last hurdle with Pope Pius XII's pronouncement "Provida Mater Ecclesia," in 1947, which recognized the members of the institutes as religious and endorsed the whole movement.

The first institute to be approved specifically after the Pope's intervention was the Sacerdotal Society of the Holy Cross and Opus Dei, better known by the last two words in its title. Founded by Father Escriva de Balaguer in 1928, the institute rapidly spread from Madrid throughout the Spanish-speaking world. It consisted of two sections, one for men and one for women. A sprinkling of secular priests was included, hence the term Sacerdotal in its title. Its primary aim was to foster the practice of Christianity among the intellectual classes especially, but the members penetrate all classes of society in an attempt to teach by example and personal interaction. The Opus Dei led the way in finding a way to include married persons in an auxiliary membership, thus indicating what may become the newest direction in religious life.

If our résumé of religious life throughout the centuries has demonstrated anything at all, it is that a continual process of adaptation is at work. It is impossible to locate the germ of change in society, suffice it to say that change begets change. The reasons may be due to mass population movements, conditions of geography or climate, industrial and technical developments, scientific discoveries, shifts in the power structure, or whatever. It has been called progress, evolution, determinism on one hand and retrogression on the other.

In any case, the subtle changes occur, perceptive leaders discover what is happening and seek to meet the new conditions. The process is true of all institutions, political and economic, as well as religious. It is also true that the establishments resist change, and that a lag occurs while the masses are educated to the new fact of life. Americans, for example, are going through a traumatic experience in trying to live a complex urban life according to the principles of a rural economy.

The history of brotherhoods has been a story of successive responses to new situations. The constants have been a conviction that what society needs is contained in the Gospels, that it is possible to imitate Christ in any age, that the vows of poverty, chastity, and obedience are the means counseled by Christ himself for those who would so follow Him, that it is more human to live this type of life in common with others who share the same motivation, and finally that it is not necessary to become a priest to do all these things.

Thus, laymen fled a pagan world into deserts, shocking it into an awareness of a new standard of values. Thus, into a crumbling world, laymen introduced an element of stability in the institution of monasticism, which devised new agricultural techniques while it preserved the records of ancient culture. Thus, laymen joined the friars in going out into the emerging towns and their universities, others cared for the sick, ransomed captives and fought for the holy places. Thus, laymen became educators and showed how the classics could be reconciled with Christianity in a new humanism. Thus, laymen joined with priests in the new clerical orders which aggressively defended Catholic Christianity against the Protestant reformers. Thus, laymen became schoolmasters to a new bourgeois class in the eighteenth and nineteenth centuries. And, thus, laymen are today intermingling with other laymen, living the life of the ancient vows in the new monastery of the world.

Our story would be neater and simpler if the older forms of religious life would automatically disappear when a new one seemed better able to answer the needs of the day. The fact is, they do not. They not only continue to exist, but they seem to flourish. The ancient Benedictine Order numbers 11,500 monks today. There are 1557 Cistercians, and 4270 Cistercians of the Strict Observance, or Trappists. The unchanging, ascetic Carthusians number 587.

The Mendicant Orders are very much a part of the contemporary scene. The Franciscans are still the largest order, there are 26,320 Friars Minor, 4170 Conventuals, 15,138 Capuchins. The Dominicans number 9000, the Augustinians 5094, the Carmelites 6880, the Servites 1549 and the Brothers of St. John of God 2537.

The orders of priests, or Clerks Regular, which originated with the Reformation are dominated now, as then, by the Jesuits who have exceeded 34,000 members. There are also 1233 Camillians who are mainly devoted to the care of the sick, and 2317 Clerks Regular of the Religious Schools.

More recent are the Clerical Religious Congregations, associations of priests and brothers who live in community and take the three simple vows. The largest of these are of Italian origin: the Salesians of St. John Bosco, 18,750; the Redemptorists, 8312; and the Passionists, 3763; and the congregations of French origin: the Oblates of Mary Immaculate, 7236; the Priests of the Holy Ghost, 4804; the Priests of the Sacred Heart of Jesus, 2920; the Religious of the Holy Cross, 2608; and the Marists, 2320. Also numerous is the Society of the Divine Word, of Dutch origin, with 5126 members.

Other congregations are referred to as Societies of Common Life. They are associations of priests who do not take the usual vows of religion. They began in seventeenth-century France with the Vincentians, now 5425, and the Suplicians, now 629. A nineteenth-century French society, the White Fathers, now has 3163 members. There is one English foundation, the Mill Hill Foreign Missions, with 1037 members, and the American societies, 303 Paulists, and 1040 Maryknoll Missionaries.

The Lay Religious Congregations do not include priests among their members. The first in time and in numbers are the Brothers of the Christian Schools with 16,689 members. Next are the Marist Brothers with 10,068. The Christian Brothers of Ireland have 3500 members, there are 3126 Brothers of the Sacred Heart, 2220 Brothers of Christian Instruction of Ploermel, 1903 Brothers of Christian Instruction of St. Gabriel, 1580 Brothers of Charity, and 1023 Brothers of the Blessed Virgin Mary.

The reason why all these religious orders of men have lasted is that they have succeeded in adapting to changing needs while maintaining an essential uniqueness which sets them apart. If they fail to serve a worthwhile purpose, they die out simply because no new vocations are attracted to an obsolete organization. If they fail to maintain the reason for their separate existence, they merge with a larger order of similar purpose.

The long-range prospect would seem to be for some sort of

massive amalgamation of religious orders. As each of them searches today for its role in the *aggiornamento* of the Church, the answer lies in how each can put the Church at the service of the world. Modern conventions, associations, communications, summer institutes, and the plethora of excellent religious literature serve to lessen traditional distinctions among orders. The external adaptations in the religious habits will result in greater uniformity in dress.

The religious orders welcome the challenge of adaptation. They willingly share society's great torment, how can man avoid self-destruction? More, how can he achieve a good life, free from want and fear? They are not at all confident that they can spell out the answers that will comfort a frightened world, but they know that the answer lies deep within the mystery of the Christian message.

CHAPTER V

The American Tradition: In Colonial America Few Brothers, but Much Brotherhood

Brotherhoods are old and honorable institutions, with a definite role in the world scheme of things. How compatible are they with the American way of life, though? Some of them seem so medieval; and almost all are European in origin. How could the life of the vows be lived in this country?

As a matter of fact, all our institutions are European in origin, frontier hypotheses notwithstanding. There is only a matter of adjustment. American religious could not accept a caste system, for example, as easily as could Europeans who were reared in a class-conscious tradition. Nor could Americans take to a life of strict discipline, or of unquestioning obedience in the same way as their European confreres.

However, there are other qualities in the American grain which account for the continued growth of the brothers. One does not have to search far for evidence of a tendency of Americans toward corporate activity. Equally persistent has been a deep-flowing religious current, a disposition to lend a helping hand, an optimism which causes us to believe that there are no ills in society which cannot be cured if we put our minds to it.

The early settlers of Jamestown lived almost like a religious community; there were no women, the men worked together, were required to offer prayers regularly during the day, ate in community and were not permitted to own private property. The difference between them and a group of religious was in the motivation, not in exterior discipline.

The Pilgrims who signed the Mayflower Compact had many of the characteristics associated with religious life. An important exception was that the Pilgrims were married. As in early Jamestown, property was owned in common, obedience to the Governor and his council was strictly required, modest dress was prescribed and a strict prayer schedule was adhered to.

During the colonial period, town meetings preserved the tradition of fraternity and responsibility in a common enterprise. This was true at least of New England. In the South a different kind of community evolved, with fewer aspects of the kind of brotherhoods we have been describing. The plantation system was a corporate activity, but the nearest approach to a common life was lived by the slaves.

It is easy to find symptoms of a disposition toward a religious life. It is not so easy to locate actual religious brothers during the colonial period. One reason is that there were a mere handful of Catholics in America then, only 25,000 Catholics by 1785.

There were, of course, strong Catholic influences at work in the French and Spanish colonies. The Franciscan Recollects and, later, the Jesuits were companions of Champlain and LaSalle in the epic exploration of the interior. Lay brothers accompanied the priests as co-workers. Brother Pacifique du Plessis was one of four Recollects who accompanied Champlain to Canada in 1615. Brother Sagard-Theodat, who came a few years later, was the chronicler of the first penetrations of the interior. Jean LaLande was martyred with Father Isaac Jogues.

The Spanish frontier to the South was held, not by forts, but by missions, most of them conducted by the Franciscans. A remarkable forerunner of all those brothers engaged in educational activities was a Franciscan named Peter of Ghent who built a school behind the Church of the Conventuals in Mexico City. In 1531, the Bishop of Mexico City wrote this tribute:

> The Herculean labors of this lay-Brother arouse in us the profoundest admiration. Without resources other than his indomitable energy, which was born of flaming charity, he built, and for many years, he maintained, a magnificent church, a hospital and a huge establishment which was, at the same time, a school of primary education, a college for higher education, a home for religious training, a trades-school, and an academy of fine arts; in a word, a center of civilization.

Peter of Ghent seems to have anticipated almost all the activities of a modern brother—and that by four hundred years!

Although there were not many Catholics in the English colonies, there were some, and if we look carefully we notice that there were brothers dutifully at work among them. They are seldom singled out by historians for mention, but they were there. Thus when the *Ark* and the *Dove* brought the first colonists to Maryland under the auspices of the Catholic, Cecil Calvert, there were two Jesuit priests and two brothers. Exactly what type of activity they engaged in is not clear, but it is clear that by 1640 Brother Ralph Crouch was in charge of a school which ranks with the earliest in the colonies. He, too, seems to have been a man of many talents. According to the English records he was the "right hand and solace" of the Fathers for nearly twenty years. "Being a man of some education, he opened schools for teaching the humanities, gave catechetical instructions to the poorer classes, and was assiduous in visiting the sick."

New York acquired a Catholic governor in the person of

Thomas Dongan, appointed by James II in 1682. Among the first four Jesuits he brought to America were two brothers. They opened a school in the following year which served the sons of some of the more prominent families of New York. The school did not outlive the regime of James II.

From the scraps of information we can gather, three points emerge. 1. The brothers shared the hard work, and therefore deserve the credit due it, of the missionary priests. 2. They were colleagues rather than servants of any kind. 3. Their most outstanding work was in pioneer educational work.

During the early national period, the number of American Catholics remained small and there were no significant developments in the history of religious brotherhoods. While new orders were springing up in profusion in France, Americans were forming associations, fraternities and societies of all sorts. William Ellery Channing wrote about this tendency in 1830.

> In truth, one of the most remarkable circumstances or features of our age, is the energy with which the principle of combination, or of action by joint force, by associated numbers, is manifesting itself. It may be said, without much exaggeration, that everything is done now by Societies. . . . You can scarcely name an object for which some institution has not been formed.

This gregariousness has become a trait of modern Americans; by instinct and tradition, we are joiners. Fraternal societies pledged to worthy causes have flourished for the last hundred years. The compelling force of good fellowship is as much a reason for the formation of religious communities as it is for all those other fraternal groups.

If religious brotherhoods are in the American tradition you might reasonably expect to see similar groups among the various religious denominations, and not exclusively within the Roman Catholic or Anglican Churches. In fact, there is striking evidence of this tendency. We might refer to it as experiments in religious communism.

In 1680, a group of Protestant mystics established the Lobadist community in northern Maryland which, although short-lived, owned 4000 acres of land. Better known is the Ephrata Cloister of the Pennsylvania Dutch region. A pious German Mennonite named Conrad Beissel chose a wilderness retreat in Lancaster County for prayer and study. Just as followers joined Anthony, Benedict, and Francis in their solitude, so disciples settled near Beissel. Soon they were organized into a religious community. The New Testament was their guide in temporal as well as spiritual matters. Celibacy was considered desirable and, in the earlier years, most of the members were unmarried. A Sister House was built for the women, who were organized into the Sisterhood of the Roses of Sharon, and a similar Brother House was provided for the tonsured, bearded brotherhood. The day began at five in the morning. Matins and a song service came before six; then there was work until nine, when breakfast was served. From nine-thirty to five the community labored, meeting again for a simple meal at the end of the day. The hours from seven to nine in the evening were spent in reading and study. Retiring at nine, the communities met again at midnight for another service, the fourth of the day. The two orders dressed in habits of white homespun linen.

There were no vows, and seceders from the orders settled nearby to raise families. The children were sent to be educated by the brothers and sisters. The Sunday School, founded in 1740, was the first of its kind in America. In effect, the Ephrata Cloister reenacted the history of monasticism. Land was held in common, poverty was a rule of life. The chief occupation was farming, and the wheat, wool, vineyards and garden plots were more than adequate to meet their needs. During the years of their greatest strength, the Ephratists sent out missionaries and established two or three branch communities modeled after the parent monastery. Conrad Beissel died in 1786, but Ephratists remained until the beginning of the present century. Today, the sturdy buildings stand as a memorial to a remarkable religious experiment.

George Rapp led six hundred German Pietists to western Pennsylvania in 1803. In 1805, a "Community of Equality" was formally established. Land was held in common, and Rapp required obedience of all his followers. In 1807, he decided upon the formal renunciation of marriage and married couples were separated. Five years after their arrival, an English visitor wrote:

> We were struck with surprise and admiration at the astonishing progress in improvements and the establishment of manufacturies which this little republic has made in five years. They have done more substantial good in the short period of five years than the same number of families, scattered about the country could have done in fifty. This arises from their unity and fraternal love, added to their uniform and persevering industry.

Rapp was restless and moved his community to a new location in Indiana, which he named Harmony. Ten years later he sold the entire properties to Robert Owen, the Scottish philanthropist, who wanted to start a socialist community. The Rappites built a third village, eighteen miles from Pittsburgh, named Economy. The sect declined afted Rapp's death in 1847; by 1900 there were only a half-dozen members still living.

Monastic communism was practiced by other German Pietists at Bethel, Missouri, at Zoar, Ohio, and at Ebenezer near Buffalo,

New York. However the largest and in many ways the most interesting of the religious communistic settlements in this country were the villages of the Shaker Society. These adherents of Mother Ann Lee established twenty settlements in seven states during the second quarter of the nineteenth century. They are best known for their often curious ritualistic dancing and for the simple beauty of their craftsmanship. They offer an example of an American variation of monasticism. Property was held in common, celibacy was the rule, and the only test of vocation was the Biblical statement which had drawn men into deserts and monasteries from the beginning: "If any man will come after me, let him deny himself, and take up his cross daily, and follow me."

There were three categories among the Shakers, a "Novitiate Order" for new members, who were for the time permitted to keep their property and live with their natural families, although celibacy was required of them, a "Junior Order" of unmarried people who inteded to become full members but who had not as yet given up their property rights, and the "Senior Order" made up of those who had been admitted to full membership. The working day was twelve hours long; children were adopted and educated; anyone in need was taken in and fed; a self-sufficient economy was practiced. In short, the usual characteristics of medieval monasticism were present in the Shaker villages.

There were other experiments in communal living during the first half of the nineteenth century. At least fifty "utopias" were established, most of them inspired by religious convictions. Like the ancient monasteries, they represent not so much a withdrawal from the world as an instruction in a better way of life. One of the better known of these ventures was the Hopedale Community near Milford, Massachusetts. Like some of the monasteries, it was too successful; its wealth led to its decline. Its founder, Adin Ballou, penned a wise afterthought. "It is my deliberate and solemn conviction that the predominating cause of the failure . . . was a moral and spiritual, not a financial one—a defficiency among its members of those graces and powers of character which are requisite to the realization of the Christian ideal of human society." He was not discouraged, he thought that communal living was to be the salvation of American society. The day would come when "the world is fitted by intellectual growth and spiritual elevation to live in Christian communism."

William Ellery Channing, whom we quoted earlier, was familiar with the Hopedale experiment. He regretted its failure and wrote wistfully, "I have for a very long time dreamed of an association in which the members, instead of preying on one another and seeking to put one another down, after the fashion of this world, should live together as brothers, seeking one-another's elevation and spiritual growth." His dream was the same as his contemporaries in Europe who were actually attempting to make the dream a reality.

The reformers of the Jacksonian age were overly optimistic. Americans were not going to join brotherhoods and sisterhoods, they were not going to flock to any utopian communities, society was not going to show measurable moral improvement. However, enough has been said to indicate that there was a genuine American tradition of religious communal living. When the European religious orders migrated to this country, they grafted on to this tradition.

CHAPTER VI

The Great Migration: European Brotherhoods Graft on to the American Tradition

The reason that religious orders suddenly appear in large numbers is that during the first half of the nineteenth century there was a remarkable increase in the Catholic population and a separate school system was created. In 1810 there were seventy-five thousand Catholics, only 1 per cent of the total population; in 1840, they numbered one million, about 6 per cent of the population; and, in 1860, there were three million of them, 10 per cent of the thirty million population.

During this period anti-Catholic agitation increased. In 1830, a Northern newspaper first made the assertion that the Catholic Church was serving as the agent of European governments in an effort to overthrow American democracy. From that time on the idea of a Catholic plot, secret and subversive, permeated Protestant argument. There were many variations of the supposed plot—ranging from the idea that the West might be overwhelmed by Catholic immigrants, to a rumor that the Pope himself was to come and set up his domain in the Mississippi Valley. In 1832, the Association for the Propagation of the Faith was founded in Lyons, France, and it became especially active on the frontier. The newly revived societies, like the Congregation of the Mission (Vincentians) and the lay religious institutes were especially interested in missionary work. All this was regarded with open hostility by many Protestants. Philadelphia Bishop Kendrick's complaint to city officials about Catholic children being required to use the King James Bible in public schools provided the occasion for a national anti-Catholic organization. Ninety-four Protestant ministers joined in the formation of the American Protestant Association in November of 1842, declaring that the principles of popery were "subversive of civil and religious liberty" and that they therefore were uniting to defend Protestant interests against "the great exertion now making to propagate that system in the United States." The question so inflamed feelings that a series of anti-Catholic riots broke out and Bishop Kendrick felt constrained to leave the city. Actually, he was not opposed to the use of the Bible in public schools, he wanted the Douay version to be used by Catholics.

The aggressive position taken by Bishop Hughes against Protestant influence in New York public schools resulted in the withdrawal of all aid to religious schools. When the New York nativists threatened, in 1844, to imitate the violence of the Philadelphia group, Hughes stationed armed guards around the city's Catholic Churches. In the end the clamor subsided without great damage being done.

The over-all effect of the campaign of the Native American Association, or Know-Nothings, was to cause Catholics to draw in upon themselves in a manner similar to the attitude of the European Church. The Papacy, threatened by the liberal movements in Italy, looked out from an embattled fortress upon a hostile world. The Church in Europe and America was by force of circumstance on the defensive and would remain in that posture until well into the present century. Since public schools were at best sectarian, and at worst anti-Catholic, a separate system of schools for the masses of immigrant children was the great necessity of the nineteenth century. The First Provincial Council of American Bishops meeting in Baltimore, in 1829, resolved that, "We judge it absolutely necessary that schools should be established, in which the young may be taught the principles of faith and morality, while being instructed in letters." At the second council, in 1833, a committee was set up to supervise the preparation of textbooks.

The first Catholic school, Georgetown, was begun in 1786 and taken over by the newly restored Jesuit Order in 1806. Five teaching communities of women were founded before 1840, three in the frontier state of Kentucky. During this time American bishops clamored for brothers from the new French and Belgian orders. Bishop Dubourg of New Orleans was especially active in the area of Lyons, France, where he helped organize the Society for the Propagation of the Faith. He persuaded the Vincentians and Christian Brothers to work in his diocese. In 1817, the Vincentians opened a college in St. Louis. They were replaced by the Jesuits, in 1828; the institution grew into St. Louis University. Jesuits also took over Spring Hill College in Mobile which had been founded in 1826.

The Christian Brothers brought to America by Bishop Dubourg opened a school at St. Genevieve in 1817, but they were then taken out of community and sent separately to work at mission stations. Soon discouraged, they left the order. Dubourg then tried to found a teaching brotherhood, but failed. The first successful effort of the Christian Brothers was a school in Baltimore, in 1846. They spread rapidly to New York, Brooklyn, St. Louis, Syracuse, Utica, Buffalo, Chicago, and other cities until their houses spanned the country. Bishop Hughes was instrumental in bringing the brothers to New York. "Should the experiment succeed," he wrote to Father Sorin of Notre Dame, "there is no reason why at a later period each Diocese might not have a house of its own." He thought it reasonable that the brothers should be paid, "and I will not say forty dollars which I think too little, but fifty dollars a year . . ." The good bishop was offended when the brothers asked for more money, "They wished to have a security for the establishment which I have not for my own subsistence." The pastor of the parish undertook the payment of the munificent sum of $600 a year for the first group of three brothers. A pattern was established, the brothers' schools became parochial rather than diocesan.

The first order of brothers to establish a permanent school was that of the Holy Cross. As we have seen, six brothers cooperated with Father Edward Sorin in founding Notre Dame in 1841. The Brothers of the Sacred Heart opened a school in Mobile, Alabama, in 1847. The Civil War was a serious threat to the existence of the subsequent schools in the South; the Reconstruction period was nearly as crippling.

The Franciscan Brothers began a school at Loretto, Pennsylvania. Another branch, the Franciscan Brothers of Brooklyn, opened St. Francis Academy in 1858, which developed into St. Francis College. Father Chaminade's Brothers of Mary came from France in 1849 and in the following year began St. Mary's Institute in Dayton which is today's Dayton University.

Theodore Ryken's Xaverian Brothers were expressly founded for work in America. The founder and six brothers accepted Bishop Spaulding's invitation to Louisville in 1854. Their reception was less than cordial. The Know-Nothings were especially active in Louisville that year. All but two of the brothers returned to Europe. Help was forthcoming in 1860, and growth was constant after the Civil War.

The first Marist Brothers arrived by way of Canada, opening a school in Lewiston, Maine, in 1886. They were followed three years later by the Brothers of Christian Instruction who began a school in Alfred, Maine. The Salesian Brothers arrived in 1898 in San Francisco, and the Christian Brothers of Ireland came to New York City in 1906.

The newly established brotherhoods shared the characteristics of the American Church after the Civil War. If the Church after 1820 was the Church of the immigrant, that characteristic became even more pronounced as the century grew old. Thousands of Italians, Hungarians, Poles, and Lithuanians—to say nothing of additional thousands from Germany and Ireland—poured into the country. These various groups were too nationality conscious to blend immediately into a harmonious family. There were periodic crises within the Catholic community. The perennial rebirth which Frederick Jackson Turner describes, the continuous contact with the frontier, caused Americans to be concerned with material things as necessary to survival. The Catholic Church was continually in touch with the European frontier as wave after wave of immigrants were absorbed. It is understandable that the Church was concerned with the essentials of survival. Elementary education and a strong interest in the labor movement were the chief interests of Churchmen. During the long period before the government concerned itself with urban problems, the newcomers were the responsibility of the Church. The Third Plenary Council in Baltimore made parochial schools mandatory with the result that by 1900 their number reached four thousand.

Hospitals, orphanages, and homes for the elderly—where the infirm, orphaned and aged immigrant found a friendly welcome in a religious atmosphere he had known from his earliest years—served the dual purpose of preserving the faith of the immigrant and of adjusting him to American ways. The historian Henry Steele Commager remarks, "It might, indeed, be maintained that the Catholic Church was during this period, one of the most effective of all agencies for democracy and Americanization."

During these years, the Catholic Church did not attempt to assume leadership in reforms of American life. It first had to prove that it was not a threat to the American way; it was not a foreign church. It had to be accepted, and acceptance was slow in coming. In 1887, Henry Bowers began the American Protective Association; it flourished during the next decade. Ex-priests, whether real or bogus, and so-called "escaped" nuns were eagerly received in the West and South. One of the most controversial issues in the days of the A.P.A. was that the child should receive religious instruction from his earliest years. Leaders like Cardinal Gibbons, Bishop Keane of the new Catholic University, and Archbishop John Ireland made it clear that they were not opposed to public schools but wanted religion included in the curriculum. John Ireland said, "I would permeate the regular state school with the religion of the majority of the children of the land, be this religion as Protestant as Protestantism can be. . . ." Given in the atmosphere of suspicion of the day, Ireland's proposal had no chance of success.

James Parton wrote an article in the Atlantic Monthly in the spring of 1868 in which he said that the United States had much to learn from the Catholic Church, not only from the moral content of its teaching but especially from its technique.

> If the same office is still to be performed for mankind, I think the organization that performs it will have to study deeply and long the Roman Catholic Church, and borrow from it nearly every leading device of its system, especially these three—celibacy, consecration for life, and special orders for special work.

His suggestions for brotherhoods and sisterhoods to train the national conscience were met with scorn.

The conditions of the day dictated the history of the teaching brotherhoods. The general poverty of immigrants meant that the religious orders would have to operate on the proverbial shoestring. It also meant that precious few laymen could afford to teach in Catholic schools so that education became a monopoly of the religious. The intellectual level of the schools was no higher than the clientele demanded, and that was not high. The nineteenth-century French tradition that schools were agencies for moral training, added to the American tradition of spare-the-rod-and-spoil-the-child, bode ill for the erring scholar. Discipline was swift, sure, and often heavy-handed.

There was a crisis within each order as more and more young Americans found fault with the foreign attitudes of older religious. There was also the European suspicion of the secular state. Federal aid, for example, was too radical to be considered seriously, but those who thought of it were against it. The bishops were almost unanimous in denouncing the abortive Smith-Townsend Act of 1922 which would have established an office of education of cabinet rank.

In the next chapter we will discuss the problems experienced by one teaching brotherhood as it adjusted to American conditions.

The prosperity which followed the Second World War made mass education really possible for the first time. The strongly entrenched tradition of a separate Catholic school system caused bishops and pastors everywhere to clamor for schools. The demand was far too great for the existing orders, even though they were growing rapidly. Several things happened. As laymen were hired in increasing numbers, salaries and the cost of physical improvements made Catholic schools exclusively expensive. Catholic leaders changed their minds about the desirability of federal aid. And, perhaps inevitably, new orders of brothers have been founded.

At least seven orders have been established since 1948. Bishop Mussio founded the Brothers of the Immaculate Heart of Mary to do charitable and educational work in Steubenville, Ohio. Bishop Edwin Byrne founded the Brothers of the Good

Shepherd in Albuquerque in 1951. Their motto is "Charity Unlimited" and their constitutions oblige them to engage in any work of charity or mercy the bishop might request.

The Brothers of St. Pius X were established in 1952 by Bishop John P. Treacy at La Crosse, Wisconsin. They do teaching and catechetical work. In 1956, the Brothers of the Holy Rosary were established in Reno, Nevada. According to their published brochure, their primary goal is by "teaching to make Christ a living reality to the youth of today." Interestingly enough, they have adopted the ancient Rule of St. Augustine for an ultra-modern apostolate.

The Brothers of the Holy Eucharist, founded in 1957, have their general mother house in Bunkie, Louisiana. Their apostolate is teaching. The Brothers of Charity of the Immaculate Heart of Mary were founded in 1958 and are located at Banning, California. Their particular concern is the care of emotionally disturbed boys. Finally the Brothers of Charity of Spokane were organized in 1963.

Two other postwar orders of priests and brothers are involved in social work. The Servants of the Holy Paraclete were founded in 1947 in the Archdiocese of Santa Fe for the unique apostolate of caring for priests with physical or psychological problems. Father Edward Garesche, S.J. organized the Sons of Mary, Health of the Sick, in 1952. They do medical and catechetical mission work in the Boston area.

The emergence of these nine new societies indicates a vitality within the Church, and moreover it proves that in our age as in every other the vocation of the brother exercises an attraction for young men who attempt to follow Christ's invitation. There are other inferences, too. One is that social work centering around some form of teaching is recognized as a felt need today. Another is that the new organizations are deliberately adopting the titles and habits modeled on the traditional orders.

While some of the new brotherhoods are harking back to the past in an attempt to seek roots, the congregations over a hundred years old are discarding the nonessential monastic trappings. These earlier teaching brotherhoods have expanded at a remarkable rate since 1945. The ten largest show a composite increase of 25 per cent.

A more remarkable postwar phenomenon has been the attraction which the strict contemplative life of the Trappists has exerted on young Americans. For a century, the Trappists struggled for a place in the American religious scene. Suddenly their membership grew to nearly 1000 monks, and in a period which saw nine new abbeys opened. Thomas Merton, whose books have made him the best known Trappist monk in America, suggests one explanation: Modern America badly needs the wisdom of professional thinkers, dedicated contemplatives. It is as if, in this day of over-specialization, Americans have given over their deepest inner life to braver souls who volunteer for the job. Two-thirds of the Trappists are brothers. According to their reply to a questionnaire sent by this writer, the trend is toward a disappearance of the traditional distinction between a choir monk and lay brother, and toward the simple status of monk.

Moreover, in 1951, the strictest of all the Church's religious orders established a foundation near Whitingham, Vermont. Almost all these Carthusians are brothers. They seek no compromise with the modern world. In reply to the question "What changes do you foresee in the role of the brother?" the Carthusian answer was "None."

Since 1945, there have been rumblings in those clerical orders which include brothers. The efforts to adapt the mission of the brother to new demands had led to searching reappraisals of the traditional notion of the lay brother. We will discuss this movement in a later chapter.

CHAPTER VII

The Great Migration: How One Order Made the Crossing

The story of the transplanting of the Marist Brothers reveals the difficulties encountered by all of the teaching brotherhoods.

Father Champagnat, ordained by the zealous Dubourg of New Orleans in a Lyons' church, was captivated by the idea of missionary work. As soon as he could, he sent four brothers to Polynesia. One year later, in 1837, he received a request from Father Fontbonne of St. Louis, Missouri, for brothers to open a school. The demands in France were too great, however, none could be spared. Successive superiors of the order were beseiged with requests. Finally, in 1885, the first Marist Brothers went to Iberville, Canada. Eight in all made the trip in the first year, thirteen more during the summer, and in September of 1886 nineteen more arrived. New schools in Canada were opened and the first United States foundation was made in Lewiston, Maine.

Still more requests for schools brought more brothers; in 1887 six schools and a novitiate were being conducted by forty-one brothers. These were the years of the French-Canadian migration to the New England mill towns. Like other immigrants they were intensely nationalistic; they clung to their language, their customs and to their religion. In fact, in many cases nationalism and religion were badly confused. The French had their ghettos, and so did the Poles and the Portuguese and the Irish. The Marist Brothers followed the path of French-Canadian migration. Their second school in this country was located in Manchester, New

Hampshire, in 1890. In 1892, four new schools were opened, one in Lowell and another in Lawrence, Massachusetts, and two in Franco-American parishes in Manhattan.

The language barrier was acutely felt in New York City. The superiors had been given a year to learn English as well as they could. Special tutors were hired to teach the brothers English. In 1895, a scholasticate was begun in one of the New York schools to provide college level instruction to the young brothers. The financial problem was even more acute than the language difficulty. Some brothers edited textbooks; one brother was put to the unlikely work of manufacturing biphosphate of lime.

Meanwhile, France was in the midst of another Church-State crisis. A law of 1901 curtailed the work of religious orders and a second law in 1903 secularized Catholic schools and dissolved religious congregations. This brought successive waves of refugee brothers, three hundred and seventy-four in all by 1911. Most of them found the transition from southern France to northern North America difficult to make; there was a high incidence of illness and many died prematurely.

In 1903, a degree of autonomy was achieved by the erection of a North American Province. The separation from France introduced difficulties enough, and the inclusion of Canada and the United States in the same province compounded the problems. There were two different systems of education, to say nothing of different cultures. The only solution was to split the province into two. In preparation for this move a training center had to be established in the United States. With the assistance of the Jesuits at St. Andrews-on-the-Hudson, property was purchased north of Poughkeepsie in 1905. A high school for young candidates for the Marist life was opened in September, 1906. Two years later, a novitiate was begun on a newly-acquired adjacent property to provide the second step in the normal religious training. Finally, the scholasticate was removed from New York City to its permanent location in Poughkeepsie.

When the American Province was separated from the Canadian in 1911, it contained twelve schools extending from Manitoba, Canada, to New York City. The province could claim ownership of only two houses, St. Ann's Academy in New York City and the training schools in Poughkeepsie where the new headquarters of the province was located. All of the other schools were parish-owned elementary schools. For their work in these schools, the brothers were paid a salary of $500 a year or less. With such an uncertain financial base, survival was something of a miracle. The first twenty years was a continual crisis: France recalled over twenty-five brothers to serve in the armed forces during World War I; some French brothers joined the United States Army; young brothers lacking adequate preparation were sent out to teach with the result that some became discouraged and left.

Meanwhile, the transition continued as the smaller schools in Canada were closed in favor of American locations. In 1919, seven brothers opened an elementary school in Savannah, Georgia. A second breakthrough was achieved when secondary levels were added to two New England schools. Another transitionary landmark was the appointment of a Canadian-born Provincial in 1922. A major step toward greater professionalism was the establishment of a junior college on the Poughkeepsie property in 1928. The level of training was a fairly accurate indication of the standards of the country as a whole. A study in 1925 reported only 25 per cent of thirty-six teaching communities had four years college training. Although only 15.4 per cent of the public school teachers had a college education, 33 per cent had a normal school training.

Still other indications of transition were petitions for the United States Province to send missionaries to the Philippines and to China. However, the Depression put an end to the missionary venture as well as to the more ambitious building programs. This proved to be the last of the great afflictions to disturb the young province; and, in spite of the continual crises, the numerical strength of the province had increased from one hundred and sixty-three brothers to two hundred and seven.

After 1930, the trend toward secondary education increased. Ten new schools were opened in a twenty-year period, during which the number of brothers doubled. The newcomers were all Americans, of course, about equally divided between "French" New Englanders and "Irish" New Yorkers. The Junior College in Poughkeepsie became a four-year liberal arts college under the name Marian, and later Marist, College. The master's degree became the goal of all teachers, and a sprinkling of doctorates began to appear. Signs of maturity were the appointment of an American-born Provincial in 1942, and the sending of the first missionaries to the Philippines in 1948.

The period after World War II was one of great expansion for the Marists, as it was for all orders of brothers, whether in teaching or in other work. New schools were opened in the South and Mid-West, brothers went to Japan and Malaysia, grammar schools were gradually closed, laymen were employed to handle the larger numbers of students.

Marist College in Poughkeepsie was opened to lay students in 1957; within seven years it had burgeoned to a student population of 1400 in day and evening divisions. The order began to conduct educational conferences and workshops; it established houses of study at Catholic University, at Rome, and in Fribourg, Switzerland. Summers were increasingly given over to theology institutes or other professional studies. In 1959, the province was divided into two, and each new one continued the remarkable postwar rate of growth. Including the missions, 686 Marists work in sixty-one houses. Plans are underway for the creation of a third United States Province in 1968.

CHAPTER VIII

Responding to the Call: How Men Decide to Become Brothers

Of real interest to anyone who might be considering the life of a brother as a career is an introduction to some people who have gone through the same experience. Of course, each person is unique and a decision such as this is one of the few that he will have to reach all alone, in his own moment of truth. Yet, it is helpful to watch individuals going through the soul-searching process.

Each of the men we are going to consider seems to feel that Divine Providence has arranged for all things to conspire together to direct him into the religious life. Vocation is a kind of heavenly conspiracy.

> I feel that I really had very little to do with the whole decision. I can't even recall a particular day on which a decision was made. I just naturally followed the call of Christ into the religious teaching vocation with as much ease as the well-oiled Pullman follows its diesel up ahead—I can only say that Christ chose me long before I even knew Him well enough to choose Him first.

Thus wrote Xaverian Brother John Joseph Sterne. One of the crucial factors in his choice seems to have been that he was in the band at St. Mary's Industrial School in Baltimore. The band acquired a degree of fame by traveling with an alumnus of St.

Mary's, Babe Ruth, and the rest of the Yankee team of 1920. An admiration for Brother Simon, bandmaster, was the first link in the chain of events which led him into the Xaverian Order.

Or, the first impulse may have come in an atmosphere of deep religious thought. Brother Simon West, a Passionist, describes how he first felt that attraction of Christ which is the call to the religious life. He was a salesman, engaged to be married, and a religious vocation was farthest from his mind. One Lenten day he and his fiancée attended services in a Passionist monastery in Pittsburgh.

> The preacher took for his text the words of Our Lord in Gethsemane to his sleepy aspostles, "Could you not watch one hour with Me?" And I could not get the question and the picture it provoked out of my mind. More and more the question seemed to be addressed to ME. More and more Our Lord appeared to be looking at ME and asking ME. Yet if anyone had told me that within a few months I would be watching an hour with the Master at two o'clock every morning in a Passionist monastery, and that I would have continued to do so until the end of my life I would have laughed at him and said, "Don't be fantastic."

In both cases there is the conviction that a personal Christ is interested. There is the same intimate invitation "Come, follow Me" that has been upsetting young men's plans since the first monks fled into the deserts.

> God could have chosen any one of a thousand different ways, but he deigned to use one of His priests in my case,

wrote Brother Alexis Norton of the Missionary Servants of the Most Holy Trinity.

> When His call first came to me through the lips of that priest in the confessional, it was as if a whole new world had opened before my gaze. As I have said, I was happy in the Navy and I was perfectly content in my state of life. I was on good terms with God, and when the thought of my eternal salvation entered my mind, I felt safe in the knowledge that I was not doing anything to endanger it seriously. My entering religious life was no dramatic conversion of a hardened sinner; rather it was a step from a good life to the best life.

Brother Norton does the same kind of work now that he did for five years in the Navy, administrative work such as bookkeeping and correspondence, but he works for a different boss and with a different motivation.

The idea of a personal, secret call is only part of the "calling of a brother." Another essential idea is the rather flattering one that "I really do make a difference." God needs me. There are certain things that I can do, certain people that I can influence. There are certain talents and skills that only I have. Much depends on how I choose to use my peculiar qualities.

Brother Henry Virgil expresses the thought neatly,

> Although I do not jump up and down with glee because I find some uneducated people to whom I can teach religion, I still have enough of the spirit of zeal and adventure to see that maybe I may do some good for the cause of Christ. I guess the deal amounts to this: there are souls to save and unless I save them they may not be saved.

Brother Henry is a Christian Brother who volunteered for work in the Philippines. As he says "I have a great deal of work to do. By this time tomorrow about 80,000 pagans will die."

Sometimes the idea of becoming a brother will occur in a sudden illumination. It just seems compellingly right. Generally this inspiration, if we can call it that, comes after there has been a good deal of spadework. Subconscious influences have been at work.

Brother Philip Harris, a Franciscan Brother of Brooklyn, tells how it happened to him.

> Just after the mid-term examinations during Our Lady's month, our class was brought to the auditorium for a vocation talk by a teaching Franciscan Brother. Bang! That was it! I don't remember what he said, but I do know that this concept of a religious career for Christ struck me forcefully.

The same thing happened to Passionist Brother Simon West, who liked most things about monastic life, but who did not particularly want to be a priest. His guide pointed out two boys who were studying to be brothers.

"Brothers! The word hit me like a blow. I turned to him and almost shouted: 'Brothers! What are brothers?' "

"They are our cooks and tailors and nurses and jacks-of-all-trades," he was informed. "We couldn't get along without them."

"As he went on talking" Brother West recalled, "I kept saying the one word 'brother' over and over. . . . Father, I said, I want to become a brother . . . just as soon as I can."

"If God wants you," came the reply, "He will easily find a way for you to get to Him."

The first mental roadblock in the way of becoming a brother is the assumption that the brothers are a breed of men set apart and that an "ordinary guy" should not aspire to that type of life. One of the most pleasant and at the same time most necessary discoveries is that the brothers are human. Not only that, they are generally very nice people. There are reasons for this generalization. Brothers try to be truly human, knowing that you have to behave as a human person before you can be a Christian or a brother. Someone who acts through impulse rather than through a process of thinking, for instance, would not be acting in a human way. One of the objectives of a brother's education is to discover what it means to be a mature person. Most continue to discover new insights all their lives. There is this freshness of a continued pursuit of knowledge about brothers.

There is also an atmosphere of charity about them. There is a conscious effort to think of others in the community, an unselfishness about them. They are usually more generous than is good for them, because they will agree to help anyone who asks. This means that their lives are overcrowded with good deeds; they have little time for private relaxation. Those who are not charitable and who are not likely to become so are advised not to remain in the religious life, usually this happens during the time of their training.

Brother Philip Harris accurately pictures community life; he was talking about his own Franciscan companions but he might have been describing any of the other religious families.

> Life with a group of religious men proved to be a stimulating experience. There was no obnoxious piety, for these men were not angels, but ordinary men striving to become saints. Dwelling in an order showed the hardships and trials stemming from rules, regulations and human frailty. But these were more than compensated for by the spirit of the order, and its men who were distinguished by their simplicity and joyfulness and detachment from worldly things, all qualities of a true Franciscan. Living with sharp minds and wits was a daily challenge to one's funny bone and sense of humility. In community life there appeared to me to be a solidarity, a

security, a stimulation. Perhaps it can be best understood by those who have been in the armed forces and learned to appreciate companionship and comradeship under stress and gunfire.

Another reason for the charitable quality of the brothers' lives is that they have to like people in the first place or else they would not consider such a life. Their love of God and love of their fellow men gets so mixed up that they can't tell one from another. Anyhow, the wholesome joy of comradeship is a fact about brothers' lives, and it is another of the pleasant discoveries awaiting anyone who becomes a brother.

Young men judge a job by what it does to the men in it. When they see that brothers generally are likeable persons, they are favorably inclined to try the same kind of life. After the usual candidate discovers that he likes the brothers and their life, his next problem is the doubt that he is capable of doing the job. You have to have the necessary intelligence; you have to be healthy; you have to have your fair share of common sense. You have to be able to do at least one of the many tasks necessary to the proper functioning of a complicated organization. There is a famous medieval story about a juggler who performed his repertory of tricks before a statue of Our Lady. It was the only skill he had. One day the statue smiled. Juggling is not much in demand these days, but almost any other talent can be employed within the religious life.

Donald H. Drees was a sportswriter for thirteen years with the *St. Louis Globe-Democrat* and the *Star-Times*. He began his career in 1934 by traveling a month with the colorful "Gas House Gang," Frankie Frisch, Dizzy and Paul Dean, Leo Durocher, Rip Collins and Pepper Martin. He got to know the top sports personalities, and led a life that most people would envy. But he, unaccountably, was not satisfied.

I knew there was no longer any desire for dates, parties, nightclubs, cocktail lounges, swank meals, big-shot affairs. Television was an irritation. Radio was almost as boresome. Newspaper headlines of crime, disaster, intrigue, became a daily dose of negatives.

After being led through the usual contrived situations which Providence arranges in these cases, Donald Drees discovered what he had been searching for. He is now Brother Dismas Drees, a Benedictine, engaged in the kind of activity the Benedictines have always done, the apostolate of the printed word. His is a good example of how it is possible to turn one's natural abilities to a religious purpose.

Another illustration of changing bosses rather than jobs is the case of Bob Rastall of Portersfield, Wisconsin. Bob was a good farmer and determined to become a better one by studying agriculture at the University of Wisconsin. He began to realize that a good farmer could be the best teacher in underdeveloped countries. He admired the dedicated work of the Divine Word Missionaries. One thing led to another, as things do, and Bob entered the Divine Word Seminary at Techny, Illinois. After six months he received the religious habit and the name Brother Mark. Two years later he pronounced his first vows. His assignment was to take charge of a huge dairy farm at Kellyville, Australia, and to train other missionaries for work in the South Pacific area.

Or take the case of Brother Alphonsus Crowley. He was jolted out of the usual teenage routine by a draft notice in August 1943. He chose the Navy and was assigned to the Hospital Corps. In June of 1944 he went to the Pacific with the Fleet Marine Force. On the way to Okinawa the chaplain asked him if he had ever thought about entering the religious life. The idea followed him from Okinawa to China. Just possibly, he thought, he might be interested in a nursing order. Coincidentally, he came upon a magazine notice about the Alexian Brothers. He clipped it out and saved it.

After the war he decided to become a registered nurse. He was delighted to find that the Alexian Brothers conducted a school of nursing. Again one step led to another and today he is both a registered nurse and an Alexian Brother, Supervisor of the Geriatrics Division at his community's sanitarium in Oshkosh, Wisconsin.

Most young men who join the religious life do so after high school, before they have acquired a professional skill. The usual indicator of success in their case is how well they have acted during high school. If they learned how to study; if they had the will power to stay with a job until it was finished; if they developed a sense of loyalty to their friends and their school; then they will probably be a success as a brother. Another very important factor is the kind of home life the young man had. There should be that security and sense of belonging which an atmosphere of love engenders.

Finally there has to be the one essential ingredient which has always been a qualification for a genuine vocation. Every brother throughout the ages and in every order has made a deliberate response to the invitation of Christ. If the day should ever come that Christ loses that special appeal He exercises over the hearts of men, then brotherhoods would break up. Another way of putting it, we could not talk about the calling of a brother unless Christ does the calling.

In a capsule, Christ came to spread the good news of God's love for man. He founded His Church to continue His work. All Christians are called to live the Christian life and by their example to spread it throughout their own private world. Brothers are professionals in that their full-time employment is to relate the timeless message of the Gospels to the specific time in which they are living. The redemption of the world is a gradual process; brothers attempt to hasten the process a bit. They share a conviction that in the end Christ will have His way. Everything and everyone will be His. That is why no task is so trivial that it cannot be consecrated by the brother who does it. The very fact that a religious dedicates himself to a certain task is a reminder to others that this task has spiritual values. The brother who is a farmer is a sermon to other farmers. Brothers who are teachers are a constant reminder to their lay colleagues that theirs is a holy calling that all of them are in the sacred business of shaping men's destinies.

Theologians have written learned treatises about the nature of vocation, about the interior versus the exterior attraction, about which state of life is the most perfect and about the obligation of following vocations. It is probably important that the theologians get their definitions right, but for our purposes their theories are not very helpful.

We will quote just one, happily a fairly simple definition of the signs of a vocation.

> They are two: (a) the absence of impediments, and (b) the firm resolution with the help of God to serve Him in the religious life. Perhaps you will demand also a certain inclination of the will. But we maintain that this inclination unless it be identified with the right intention is something that cannot be clearly defined and can only give rise to useless doubts and mistakes. For your hearer will probably understand this inclination to mean that natural relish or desire which is only too often wanting in the best of vocations.

In other words, there doesn't have to be a "natural relish," but there does have to be a firm resolution. We might try to summarize what we have said about vocations thus far.

1. A man learns about Christ.
2. He realizes that Christ's work still goes on in the world.
3. He sees the need of promoting this work.
4. He knows that he is capable of doing it.
5. He is convinced that his decision will make a difference in how Christ's plan is carried out.
6. He makes up his mind to do his best to do the job.
7. He is accepted by the authorities of a particular religious order.

We must be careful not to give the impression that a vocation is a clearly definable, once-and-for-all sort of thing. The crucial fact about a vocation is that it has to be lived. The commitment has to be continual.

CHAPTER IX

Becoming a Brother: What the Training Is Like

A generation ago most of those who joined the religious life did so during high school. In fact, in the days when brothers concentrated on working at the elementary level, most of their vocations came right out of their own schools. However, with the shift to secondary and higher education, religious orders increasingly seek older candidates.

Many of the teaching brotherhoods are in the process of reducing the length of their secondary training schools, or juniorates. Several have dropped the juniorate completely, some are being phased out. In one or two cases however the juniorates are being expanded.

The juniorates serve a useful purpose where there are enough candidates to justify a separate high school staff and facilities. They are valuable in that young men can begin orienting their life at an earlier age towards their lifework. The value of the spiritual development in this stage is difficult to assess, but it is generally considered to be significant. The trend in religious juniorates is toward greater individual responsibility and less external restriction. The atmosphere is more that of a modern high school than that of a junior monastery. However, there is a family spirit and attention which even the best high schools cannot afford.

The reasons which lead younger people into the religious life are understandably less mature than those of high school graduates or older men. Thus some youngsters will like a certain brother and will join the order to be more like him. Some might like the idea of boarding away from home. Others might go because their friends carry them along. One young man said he joined because he wanted a chance to play basketball and the juniorate had a new gym. The reasons that bring such young men into religious life are not nearly as important as the reasons that cause them to stay. By the time they complete their juniorate education they should have convictions which they can build upon.

After the juniorate comes the novitiate, the heart of all religious training. During the juniorate the students go home during the summer months and at other times. They dress and act much like other students of high school age. But the novitiate represents a deliberate attempt on the part of the religious orders to introduce a new element into the lives of their recruits. The novitiate is more a religious experience than it is a school. The graduates of the juniorate join the young men from other high schools and some from college in the first phase of the novitiate training, the postulancy. The postulant, as the name implies, is one who is in the condition of asking for admission to the order. He continues to wear his ordinary clothes and he may engage in college studies. The length of this period varies from one order to another more than any other aspect of religious training. The two extremes are two months and one year. Six months is the usual length of the postulancy for most orders.

When the novice year begins, there is a definite change of emphasis. Brother David Ottmar, Novicemaster at the Marist Novitiate in Tyngsboro, Massachusetts has explained the purpose of this year.

> From the start newcomers to the novitiate are expected to open their eyes to the life we live. We do not snow them

under with directives. We strive to have our young men move as much by hard-earned and personally comprehended values as by detailed rules and regulations, with the use of authority not exceeding its proper place in a society of free men. No doubt but that in this there is a danger to authority and obedience, as traditionally understood. However, it is most important to understand and to teach that man's most steady and important obedience is to God's Providence. . . . We must teach them to be outgoing toward life, toward reality; we must teach them to love, to respond. Responsibility is perhaps our most important novitiate product; it is essential groundwork for progress in all fields of formation.

Today's novitiates are isolated physically, but they are very much attuned to the dynamic spirit at work in the Church. They employ the latest insights of psychology and sociology as well as of theology. Directors of novices are urged to grasp as completely as possible the background of each candidate. They have a deep insight into the theory of temperament, personality and character. Further, the director and staff of the house of formation are aware of the relationship between the religious vocation and the professional activity of the order. The only way for religious congregations to be of service is to be at least as professional as are lay people engaged in the same activities. To an increasing degree professional persons, lay and religious, who have demonstrated a high degree of accomplishment precisely as eminently qualified professional people are being called upon to talk to the novices about such professional living and its implications for the Church, for students, and for the effectiveness of the congregation. Too frequently in the past, this aspect of the religious life was neglected. In some cases there was an assumption that the really important part of the life was the time set aside for formal prayer. The work done otherwise was a kind of distraction, a necessary evil. Fortunately this attitude has disappeared, and the religious realizes that he can serve God equally well through other men, through his work or through his community life. Professional and religious accomplishment build upon, and depend upon, each other.

The brother continues his spiritual and professional development in a post-novitiate house usually called a scholasticate. These houses may be independent institutions, or they may be situated on the campuses of colleges. The various brotherhoods are careful to give their young members the best educational opportunity. The level of academic achievement has steadily risen with the years and almost all teaching orders require a college degree before the young men begin their work in a classroom.

The young brothers generally study for their graduate degrees and teach at the same time. There is a tendency today to provide time for study in the better graduate schools of the United States and Europe for capable young brothers.

CHAPTER X

Becoming a Brother: An Autobiography

The best way of explaining the educational development of a brother is to take a typical case and follow him from step to step. Rather than attempt to create a fictitious character, allow me to relate what happened to me.

I attended Aquinas High School, then called Boys' Catholic High School in Augusta, Georgia. I liked the brothers themselves and I liked the work they did. The school was a powerful influence on my life and on the lives of my classmates. It was a new school and we were pioneers. Perhaps that may have had something to do with it. We were underfoot so much the brothers put us to work, painting mostly. To get us to work and to make us enjoy it was a phenomenon, considering that we Southerners had formerly conscientiously avoided all forms of manual labor. It was a small school; there were only twenty-five in my graduating class. All the Catholic boys in Augusta were in the school, but there were not many Catholics in Augusta. In fact there were more Catholic boys in one of our large New York high schools than there were in the entire state of Georgia. So we had a large sprinkling of non-Catholics. They, too, sat in on the religion lessons. One of my classmates was a transfer student with an unlikely name for a student in a Catholic school, Luther Calvin Snellgrove. I could tell he was doing some hard thinking one day in class; he turned to me with a puzzled frown. "How could all these men be brothers when they don't even look alike?" I tried to explain that Marist was not their family name, but the name of their organization.

No one from our school had gone away to join the brothers and the novitiate in Poughkeepsie seemed a world away. I didn't know what to expect. One of the brothers mentioned, rather grimly, I thought, that it would be tough. I expected the worst. I would not have been surprised if they had put me to work digging graves. However, the brothers I knew seemed to have survived the ordeal, they were healthy, happy and as normal as could be desired. If they could endure the rigors of the novitiate, then so could I. I remember that although I was reasonably sure I wanted to become a brother, I was not absolutely sure. At least I was sure that I wanted to want to become a brother, and had to settle for what might be referred to as certitude one step removed.

The problem of what to pack was a thorny one. If I could not imagine what I would be doing, then still less could I decide what to wear. Nowadays they prepare lists for such purposes, but then we had to guess. The draft board complicated things considerably. The war in Europe was over by the time I graduated in 1945, but they were still drafting people. It never occurred to me that I should enter the armed forces, because I rather felt that what I was doing was more difficult and more useful for my country. Therefore I had to avoid being drafted by leaving for Poughkeepsie at least a month before my eighteenth birthday in July. That meant that I would be at the novitiate three months before the rest of my group arrived. It also meant that I would undergo what must be the longest novitiate on record. However, I do not doubt that I needed every minute of it. There was a succession of farewell parties, many late-hour "discussions," many good-byes, tearful and otherwise, many explanations on my part of what a brother was, and many "last-times" while waiting out the count-down.

My first impression of the novices and postulants was that I had never seen such a friendly bunch. They were more than friendly, they were downright charitable. They seemed bent on outdoing each other in all manner of kindnesses. There was one difficulty, I could not always understood their northern accents, especially when they engaged in lightning-like repartee. Gradually I grew not only to understand my classmates, but to talk like them. I learned to pronounce an "r," and to say "I" with two syllables instead of one long one.

Our Master of Novices was an unforgettable personality, Brother Henry Charles. The novitiate was impregnated with his character, which was a shade tougher than that of a Marine sergeant. He was definitely of the no-nonsense school. I am quite sure that he wanted to see how we could stand up under pressure, that he wanted us to discover our flaws of character, that he wanted us to grow from boys into men. Anyhow, he never lost an opportunity to reveal to us the error of our ways. Furthermore, since he seemed to be present at various places at the same time, no fault ever went undiscovered. . . . We were not pampered and the novitiate was definitely not a democracy.

There were many aspects of our novitiate days that have changed. I remember a number of features traceable to our French founders. Reading at one of the meals was in French and we were supposed to speak French for a while during the evening recreation. Showers were used much more sparingly than today. The water pressure in the rambling wooden building was not what it should have been and the showers were utterly unreliable. You might be frantically soaping as precious moments ticked away when the spray would suddenly subside into a trickle. We learned to accept such frustrations as part of training.

Work periods were an important part of our lives. Since we did not budge from the novitiate grounds for two entire years the property was well-manicured. During the war we supplied most of our own needs by operating a farm. In fact, the novitiate and the farm were so interrelated that it was hard to tell where one left off and the other began. Brother Henry, whose title was Brother Master, thought nothing of announcing that we would spend this afternoon's recreation weeding strawberries. Never have strawberries received such tender care as he gave ours. We also weeded stringbeans, corn, rhubarb and sundry other crops. Accidents happened. Brother Henry told an eager group of postulants to weed the rhubarb and they pulled out every last rhubarb plant. He would usually give out the work assignments in a common room called the oratory. There was a caste system about it, certain jobs were prestigious, others seemed to be for the purpose of teaching humility. Chopping down trees, for instance, was highly rated. Unknotting string was an ignominious assignment, an indication that that particular novice was considered at least unskilled and perhaps incompetent. Brother Henry was not one to waste words in giving directions. He would wave his hand in the direction of the forest behind the novitiate and say "Chop down that tree." One felt like a simpleton if he asked which tree.

The daily program included morning prayers and Mass, breakfast during which someone read aloud, "employments" such as sweeping, raking, washing dishes, or similar clean-up operations, class, dinner (again with reading), and a period of recreation. This would be the first opportunity all day to talk to one another. After reciting part of the Office of the Blessed Virgin we would have either work, recreation or more class. Before supper there would be another part of the Office and spiritual reading aloud for fifteen minutes. More reading during supper. A short recreation period, an hour's "secular study," then evening prayer and early to bed. Since we were in silence such a large part of the day, we became excessively giddy during some of the more solemn moments. Reading during the meals was a special source of merriment. Misplaced pauses would convulse the entire audience. One tense novice read "Bernadette ran up the hill and burst open—the door." Several minutes elapsed before quiet was restored. In short, the silence of the novitiate was an alert, dynamic, familial thing. We reacted as a group to any and every stimulus. Laughter was frequent, during reading, during class, and during Brother Henry's conferences. Even the time of meditation and the deep, silent moments in the chapel hid a quiet liveliness.

The recreations were occasions for letting off steam. Everybody played something or other. Even those who were not athletically inclined played, although they were isolated in right field. My first mistake was in treating these organized games as larks. I soon learned that 100 per cent college try was expected. When we played the college brothers the competition was deadly serious. We generally lost. The Brother Prefect who was in charge of the recreational aspect of our lives had to be quite ingenious at improvising tournaments and leagues of all kinds.

I was told that the novitiate would be difficult, and when I look back on it, it was. However, those two years were filled with a happiness that defies description. It was a time for discovering Christ and that was after all why we came.

At the end of the postulant year we received the religious habit, a cassock. In those days we also were given a new name. Since then the major superiors decided that the business of assigning names was more trouble than it was worth. Now the novices retain their family name. At the end of the novice year we made our first vows of poverty, chastity, and obedience for one year. We would renew these vows each year for five years before being allowed to make perpetual vows.

After the novitiate we marched to the other side of the property to begin the college phase of our training. We were now called scholastics. One other brother and myself had begun our college work during our postulant year when everyone else was engaged in their senior year of high school. As a result I had a disjointed schedule which allowed more free time than usual. I read voraciously, and learned at least as much as I would have in class. Just at this time the college received its charter from the New York Board of Regents. Plans were afoot to construct new facilities. Innumerable study sessions were interrupted by the cry of "Cinder blocks." We would bail out of the study hall, doffing cassocks as we went, unload the truck and then reassume our student's role. Ten years of construction, most of it by the brothers, were a necessary investment in the future of Marist College. By 1957 it could accommodate lay students from the area; then dormitories began to rise and the student population mushroomed to over a thousand. Those who see the college today could not imagine how it was when a handful of student brothers had to double as day laborers.

The scholasticate was an exciting time, with those intellectual excursions which are a necessary part of the college experience. We made our plans to reshape the world and wondered what the older generation had been doing, much as today's students wonder what we did. There were fewer restrictions than in the novitiate and individual responsibility was acknowledged. Yet there was not nearly so much traffic between the college and the outside community as prevails today. The world was then regarded as a dangerous, alien presence. Today this same world is replacing the concept of the classroom as a social laboratory. You go out to meet people now.

After two years' scholasticate we were permitted to visit our families. It was a big moment, our first vacation. The four years that had elapsed left an enormous chasm between my high school friends and myself. Each was carving out his own career, each had outgrown adolescence. In some ways I felt older going home the first time than any time since. Yet though we now had different interests in some strange and wonderful way, the fact that I was now a brother brought me closer to my high school friends. We have had reunions, which grow larger with the years, every time I visit Augusta. I always marvel at the success of the pioneer students at old Boys' Catholic High School. Among them are prominent surgeons, brokers, accountants, lawyers, a judge, a state senator, the state controller, a bank president, and others.

The first visit ended and I returned to New York. I had not graduated, having finished three and a half years, work during the postulant year and two years' scholasticate. I had an inkling that I would be sent out teaching, and would have to complete my B.A. work on a part-time basis. So from Grand Central Terminal in New York I called one of our New York schools and asked them if they had received the new assignments. They had. After an interminable wait my name was located. I had been assigned to teach the fourth grade at Mount Saint Michael in the Bronx. I had only the vaguest notion of New York City geography and no acquaintance at all with the intricacies of the subway system. I was about to get a taxi to drive me to Mount Saint Michael when Providence sent another Marist Brother across my path. He explained that it would cost a small fortune by taxi since Mount Saint Michael was at least twenty miles away. Then he led me through the labyrinth and into a subway car with instructions to ride to the last stop.

Mount Saint Michael was and is a huge, intricate educational mechanism. One gets the impression that it runs itself and doesn't need the help of petty mortals. I dreaded the thought of being swallowed up in such a factory system. Still, the fourth grade was not impersonal. There were twenty-five youngsters, each one unique. Most were residents, many from broken homes. Some were model children, there to get a good education, and some were authentic holy terrors sent to the brothers because no one else could tame them.

My first mistake was underestimating their intelligence. Because they were so small, I tried an approach resembling baby-talk. They immediately realized that they had an easy mark and discipline collapsed. When I tried reasoning with them they were not interested in educational theory. My sanity was preserved by a timely appendix seizure. They told me that I almost died on the operating table, but all I can remember is the blessed relief of the hospital.

Meanwhile the principal of the elementary division, a wise disciplinarian of the old school, had taken my fourth grade. When I returned he had them sitting up straight with folded arms. Their trips to the washroom were exercises in precision. Somehow the crisis had passed and my fourth-graders and I got along on a man-to-man basis thenceforward. I suspect that they felt responsible for my hospitalization and some spark of compassion had been struck. Or else they were afraid of another encounter with the principal. I am not sure whether enlightened pedagogues would agree but we made everything a contest. Even "Let's see who can keep quiet the fastest." We became expert in mental arithmetic and in all sorts of bees. Some of the techniques were equally applicable in high school. In fact I still have captains in charge of opening windows, taking care of maps, and other such aspects of classroom management.

That first year is easier to remember than any of the intervening ones, and the first class will always occupy a special place in my affections. I suppose that is the way it is with most teachers. I was at Mount Saint Michael long enough to watch my fourth-graders progress through the elementary grades and high school. I taught some of them again as seniors.

My second year's assignment was to teach world history to sophomores. I had no less than five periods of essentially the same subject matter. I developed a reputation for knowing the facts, especially in the fourth and fifth periods.

During this time I was occupied with those things which all young brothers must encounter, especially extracurricular activities and the problem of finishing my formal education. I became interested in debating and speech work, and soon found that if it was rewarding, it was equally demanding. The rewarding part was the awareness that young men were visibly growing in the ability to think clearly and to communicate their thoughts in public with poise and assurance. The demanding part was the long hours of practice. As usual, competition was the incentive as our New York Catholic Forensic League expanded and merged with the Pittsburgh league to form the National Catholic Forensic League.

The other problem which had to be coped with was the college work. With so many demands on one's time, the temptation was to let personal work slip. Then, too, we seemed to be working in a vacuum. No one knew what courses we were taking or what results we achieved. One happy result was that we became experienced in self-motivation. I finished my B.A. at Fordham's downtown branch. There were many late-evening encounters with inebriated wanderers from the bowery for whom the Roman collar is an irresistible magnet. Each subway ride was an adventure. When I began my M.A. studies it was a comparatively short trip to the main campus at Rose Hill. Having acquired the knack of it, I kept right on going for my Ph.D. Although the tendency today is to rush through the Ph.D. on a full-time basis, there was a very real advantage in going to school and in teaching at the same time. One had a chance to share new insights with the high school students. The extended time also permitted me to get around to reading at least those books which "every schoolboy has read."

After five years of temporary vows, our scattered group

reunited to make perpetual profession. A dispensation from perpetual vows is possible, but the profession is like a marriage contract; it is made for life. The only external difference was that we could now wear a crucifix upon our cassocks in addition to the cord and collar. There was the implication that we were at last accepted into full membership.

I should not end here because there were other things that happened which may be considered typical of a brother's life. As year after year slipped by, teaching became more and more rewarding. Once you become a fixture, the students give you the benefit of the doubt. Their one demand is that the teacher be prepared. There should be a sensible central point to every lesson. If possible each one should be a joint adventure by teacher and student into the subject matter, and the discovery there of new insights into the nature of man in his world.

After ten years at Mount Saint Michael, the powers that be decided to split the United States Province into two. It so happened that the Mount was not included in the same province as my alma mater in Augusta. I felt torn between loyalties, if I may strain for comparison, somewhat like Robert E. Lee weighing his decision. My original reason for joining the order had been the hope of teaching in the South where the need seemed most acute. So I elected to leave my beloved Mount Saint Michael for the other province. Unexpected things continually happen to me; one happened at this point. My new province opened a school in Miami, Florida, and I was assigned to the first faculty. Miami was not hard to take, even though it was as far from Augusta as was New York. Of course, the students had to be introduced to such concepts as homework and discipline. There were only six of us and so we were overloaded with activities. But there was a relaxed atmosphere about it all, due perhaps to the palm trees and Miami's justly famous weather, and especially because of the warm, friendly reception we received from the students and their parents. Brothers are continually in danger of being spoiled by the hospitality of nice people.

Miami's dynamic Bishop Coleman Carroll went right on opening schools, something like twelve in three years, and our Christopher Columbus High School developed a reputation for maturity before its time. The Holy Cross Brothers opened a school the year we did; they were followed by the Christian Brothers, the Marianists and by another Marist school.

While we were in Miami history was being made. I remember going to the airport with my Director, Brother Benedict, to meet some eighty Marist Brothers who had been expelled from Castro's Cuba. They were utterly lost in the confusion of Miami's International Airport. We shepherded them into our school and did what we could to make their exile less painful. Their stories will make grim reading some day, and some of these brothers were genuine heroes.

One of the highlights of my stay in Miami was the National Catholic Forensic League Tournament at the Americana Hotel in 1962. Quite a lot of planning went into that event. Two years prior there was a question of breaking up the league because it was growing too unwieldly. Sister Zoe, of the Pittsburgh Diocese and one of the founders of the National League, thought that such a move would be a backward step, and so did I. We each agreed to play host to the national tournament and thus postpone the question of division. The only problem in Miami was that there was no league in existence. We had to organize a league and with the new moderators prepare for the tournament, the major speech event of the year for several hundred of the country's top high school debaters and orators. The key factor was the Americana Hotel. The management agreed to give us eighty rooms, a fishing trip and all sorts of extras which left me dazed and delighted. This meant that for the first time the entire tournament could be conducted under one roof. Since then all the "nationals" have been staged in hotels. I received the red carpet treatment every time I went to the Americana and I went frequently enough. The tournament was a great success, and our amateur moderators conducted themselves expertly. The hotel staff co-operated beautifully. I ended up in a luxurious pool-side suite, compliments of the management. The moral of my story is that modern monks get into the darndest situations.

That was my last year in exotic Miami. After ten years of perpetual profession we have the opportunity of making a second novitiate. This five-month period of prayer and study had traditionally been done in one of the more ancient houses of the order in the southern part of France. But a kindly Providence had inspired our superiors to establish a house for English-speaking brothers in Fribourg, Switzerland. From Miami to Switzerland! From one ultimate to another. The journey to and from Fribourg was a priceless experience, of course, but the five months in the Second Novitiate was the heart of the matter. Everyone, upon reaching the age of thirty-five, should have their own Fribourg—five months snatched from a busy life-time to stop and take stock, to focus again on your goals, to catch up on the great movements at work in the Church and the world, to think and write and to talk to Christ in the vast cathedral of the mountains. Once, while gazing up in awe at the magnificence of the Matterhorn, I thought thankfully, brothers do get into the darndest places.

The second novitiate was a complete break, I had said my good-byes in Miami, and had no idea where I might be assigned. Two brothers met me as the *Carinthia* docked with news that I was to report to Marist College in Poughkeepsie, and that my first class met in two days time! Needless to say, college opened up a new world of opportunities. It is above all a world of discussion, dialogues, conversations and confrontations. You are expected to move smoothly from an historical convention to an educational conference, you are expected to fraternize with socially prominent trustees and to hob-nob with politicians, you are to be equally at ease in a faculty symposium as at a student bull session. And it is assumed that you are to be a good teacher, which of course means that you must continue to make discoveries in your own field.

The best possible advice I could give any student brother is to develop in all his capacities and be ready for anything at all. We will discuss the possibilities that confront brothers later. I have reviewed my own case history after a fruitless attempt to select a typical career. No one is typical; each is unique.

Just to give you an idea of how atypical brothers are, let me give you other examples. The first that comes to mind is Brother Leo Ryan whom I met at a college workshop in Ashville, North Carolina. Bishop Waters had assembled some of the best minds in the country for the three-week affair. There was Bishop Wright, the late dearly-loved Sister Madeleva, Anne Fremantle, Monsignor George Higgins, Joseph Fichter, S.J., Father Leo Ward of Notre Dame, and similarly gifted and famous people. Brother Leo Ryan, a Viatorian, was one of the best. At the time, he was Director of Continuing Education and Summer Sessions of Marquette University. From 1960 to 1962 he served as the National President of the Catholic Business Education Association. The Association later created a National Service Award to be called "Brother Leo V. Ryan Award" in recognition of his contribution to the organization. In 1959 he was given the "Young Man of the Year Award" by the Milwaukee Junior Chamber of Commerce. He is a member of the Governor's Committee on the United Nations, a member of the President's Committee on Employment of the Handicapped and on the Executive Board of the National Catholic

Committee on Adult Education. At the time he had written over three hundred articles on business and social science topics.

Brother Leo's achievements indicate what can be done by a capable religious who knows the meaning of responsibility. In his case he has created an unparalleled opportunity to formulate a new philosophy of business based on the dignity of the individual person. If he can give a deeper meaning to the life of an organization man, he will serve society in one of its greatest needs.

I might have cited another spectacular career. Brother Nilus Donnelly started out as a physics teacher and ended up as a general contractor of sorts. After supervising the construction of a huge gymnasium at Central Catholic High School in Lawrence, Massachusetts, he came to Marist College to mastermind the college expansion program. With a minimum amount of advice from professionals he constructed a succession of buildings. He bought and operated heavy equipment, such as bulldozers and cranes. Brothers supplied the manpower, and most of the work was done during their summers. If put to a vote today the brothers involved would probably not do it again. But in a manner that would have done credit to the Corps of Engineers they put up five buildings of daring design. Brother Nilus was flown to Miami to receive the annual award of the National Fenestration Society for the window design of the student brothers' study hall. Today Brother Nilus is Clerk of the Works on the $4,000,000 Champagnat Hall being built on the Marist campus under a loan from the State Dormitory Authority.

Neither Brother Leo Ryan nor Brother Nilus could have foreseen what the future held for them when they began their religious life. Nor, I would venture to say, could Brother Timothy, F.S.C. He is that genial gentleman whose picture graces the advertisements for Christian Brothers wine, for he is Cellarmaster of the Christian Brothers Wine and Champagne Cellars in St. Helena. One of his brochures resembles a hard-sell approach to the recruiting of vocations. It reads "You too can become a Wine Taster." Actually it turns out to be only a five-minute course in wine tasting, not an inducement to emulate Brother Timothy.

CHAPTER XI

Brothers in the Future: Where are They Going?

It is only natural that anyone who seriously considers a specific career ask what direction that career is moving. There is no doubt that the brother's career is changing. The brothers themselves are the agents of change; they understand that they cannot expect Rome to spell out their role in the modern world. The last session of the Vatican Council supplied a word of encouragement in its schema on religious.

> This renovation shall preserve the nature, the scope, and the special spirit, as well as the sound traditions which make up the patrimony of every institute. The whole tenor of their life and activities must be adjusted to the physical and psychic circumstances of present day life, to the needs of the apostolate, to cultural and economic exigencies, especially in mission territories. Consequently in whatever degree they may be necessary, all Constitutions, Directories, Custom Books, Prayer Manuals, Ceremonials and other similar texts are to be carefully revised.

The *Constitution on the Church* issued by the Council endorses the brother's life, indicating that the living out of the counsels of poverty, chastity and obedience contributes in a special way to the holiness of the Church. The exact text reads as follows:

> The holiness of the Church is fostered in a special way by the observance of the counsels proposed in the Gospel by our Lord to His disciples. An eminent position among these is held by virginity, or the celibate state. This is a precious gift of divine grace given by the Father to certain souls whereby they may devote themselves to God alone the more easily due to an undivided heart. This perfect continency, out of desire for the kingdom of heaven, has always been held in particular honor in the Church. The reason for this was and is that perfect continency for the love of God is an incentive to charity and is certainly a particular source of spiritual fecundity in the world.

The Council Fathers tell us that through religious men and women the Church presents Christ daily to all types of men, believers and unbelievers alike. The function of all religious is to bear witness to Christ in as many of the facets of His life as possible. Religious are an outward sign signifying that there is another standard of values than that adopted by suburbia.

In an article in the Graymoor publication, *The Lamp,* Father William Hogan, C.S.C., analyzes the position of the brother today.

> Brothers of today are building up the Body of Christ here on earth by the faithful living of their religious vows, thereby vitally contributing to the sanctification of mankind. They have emerged and are emerging farther still from their obscure position of the Middle Ages and assuming the place that is rightfully theirs in bearing witness before all mankind to the mission of Christ in this world. The "Brother Juniper" type of brother is fast disappearing, and rightfully so. He is giving place to the original conception of what a brother was meant to be.

Brothers are moving into positions of influence and leadership in their various professions. More and more are receiving degrees in Sacred Theology and Canon Law, fields formerly reserved to priests. Brothers are playing an important part in formulating a fresh approach to the teaching of religion. Their colleges are recognized as institutions of excellence and brothers who are college administrators are occupying important positions in national educational organizations. Some brothers are certified accountants and the chief fiscal officers in large institutions, familiar with investment practices and the intricacies of high finance. Brothers are the chief fund-raisers and public relations officers at some of their institutions. Some are leading architects of religious buildings and some are internationally known scientists. They conduct hospitals and schools of nursing. They have entered the communications media and operate printing shops and radio stations. Some have become expert psychologists and counselors. Brothers in charge of the food services in large institutions have become authorities in their fields, conducting workshops and summer institutions for the personnel of both religious and secular institutions. They have appeared as speakers at national restaurant association meetings and at conventions for the food service industry.

Books and magazine articles by brothers on professional and spiritual topics are multiplying. There is an ecumenical spirit at work among the various orders which is manifest in the publication of the *Brothers' Newsletter* in conjunction with the Brothers' Panel of the Mission Secretariat. Brother Damian Carroll, a Passionist, is editor; he states the theme of the magazine in one of his editorials.

> Now today the vocation of the religious brother has taken on a fresh appearance and is well on its way to shaking off

the dust of old world monasticism, having accepted the challenge of the aggiornamento sweeping the Church.

As though to emphasize the spirit of co-operation, the assistant editors of the *Newsletter* are a Graymoor Brother and a Jesuit; the printing is done by a Salvatorian Brother.

Brother Basil O'Leary, F.S.C., is one of those breaking into print. In a recent article in *Commonweal* he analyzed the nature of the brother's calling. The fullness of Christian witness requires diverse ways of life, he says, one is that of the layman who is uniquely called to an exaltation of family love and political involvement. "The other is that of the religious who 'gives up' these high values of life as a sacramental revelation of the eschatological role of temporal existence. This is the brother's way of salvation as well as his claim to distinctive ecclesial 'place.' " In other words the religious preaches in a wordless sermon that the normal standard of values is not necessarily the eternal standard of values.

The adaptation of the brother's life is perhaps more complicated in the clerical institutes. Here also the Vatican Council's schema for religious has applied a stimulus and a guideline. "To strengthen the bonds of brotherhood, those known as lay-religious or others of a similar category should be given a closer share in the life and activities of the institute." In short, class distinctions should be eliminated in those orders which include both priests and brothers. About half of the brothers in this country are members of clerical orders. They face the problem of overcoming customs of long standing and in some cases constitutional distinctions between priests and brothers.

Brother Paul Henry of the Oblates of St. Francis De Sales has recently conducted a survey of brother formation techiques in clerical communities. He notes a definite trend toward greater specialization. Post-novitiate training includes increased emphasis on moral theology, liturgy and Scripture. Secular subjects include advanced mathematics courses, philosophy and psychology. The technical courses prepare brothers for various trades such as cooking, carpentry, masonry, kitchen administration. Many communities send their brothers out to various shop and trade schools. There is also a trend toward increased cultural opportunities during this training period. He notes that while in a few orders the brothers still say "Paters and Aves" or the Office of the Blessed Virgin, many have already changed to a shortened form of the Breviary in English. In many cases the brothers recite parts of the Office with the clerics. Brother Paul concludes his study with the remark "It seems to be quite evident that all communities are striving to bring their brothers up to date with the Church and the modern apostolate."

There is an advantage in a book of this sort of acquainting the reader with as many as possible of the various kinds of brothers and the general direction of the changes in this vocation. For this purpose I wrote to the superior of each order asking him to indicate briefly the kind of work his brothers did and any changes he might foresee. Each answer gives an insight into the spirit of the order.

One of the more extensive replies was submitted by Brother Conrad, Vocational Director of Franciscan Brothers. Brothers in his community engage in manual work and teaching. His comment on the future requires direct quotation.

> For some decades now the brother's vocation has lain like a sleeping giant whose strength has never been completely called upon. The renewal in the Church calls for just such a vocation to function in the Body of Christ. Brothers are religious and dedicated long-time career men for many non-

> sacramental roles in the Church. The Church has need of such men who will bridge the many gaps between the world and the religious life with God.

He notes the increased interest, the emphasis on training, the stricter screening of candidates and the increase in vocations as significant indications that

> the day will come when the number and quality of the men called to this vocation will present a renaissance unknown in history.

Father Matthew of Gethsemani Abbey in Kentucky replied that Trappists did all sorts of manual work, cheesemaking, farming, dairying, carpentry, plumbing, electricity, building, bookkeeping, shoe repair, baking, cooking, laundry, garage, and machinery repair, tailoring, art, and printing. They also operate a dehydrator-pellet mill, whatever that might be. Such a litany of jobs is the best description of a busy monastery. The trend is toward the disappearance of the distinction between choir monk and lay-brother in favor of the simple designation "monk."

The Pauline Fathers and Brothers are a modern American order founded some fifty years ago. It offers a good illustration of the way brothers can be partners with priests in a common apostolate. They are specialists in the media of communications. Besides printing and binding both hard-bound and paperback books, the Paulines publish two magazines and a weekly supplement. For their motion picture work the society has a film center in Brookline, Massachusetts. Here the fathers and brothers handle not only the circulation of both religious and secular films, but also do the reviewing, film splicing and voice dubbing for these films. According to their talents Paulines may become any of the following: managing editors, rewrite men, designers, directors, proofreaders, artists, photographers, pressmen, binders, typesetters, photoengravers.

The Assumptionist Brothers engage in maintenance work, cooking, secretarial work and supervision of students. One brother is treasurer of a house, another is assistant treasurer. According to Father Joseph Loiselle, more brothers will assume similarly important administrative positions. They will also become involved in direct apostolic work and in teaching.

The Edmundites now accept young men who want to teach but who do not want to be ordained. Most now are in clerical work, a few are in maintenance.

Among the Capuchins brothers do the usual household chores, in addition to the singular task of sandal-making. The cooks have been trained professionally and the infirmarians have worked in hospitals. Some of them teach special catechetical classes. The direction here is clearly toward a greater participation in the Franciscan apostolate. "Everything is changing so rapidly," writes Father Juniper Rapp, Director of the Provincial Office of Public Relations in Pittsburgh.

Brothers in the Claretian Society are engaged in domestic service for the most part, but young brothers are taking courses at Indiana State University in Industrial Arts, commercial courses and Physical Education. They will be placed in management positions in their institutions.

Among the Priests of the Sacred Heart the brothers have historically engaged in domestic work and manual labor, but in recent years their field has been broadened by professional training. Brothers are on the faculty of their seminary, for example. "The horizons indeed are growing broader," writes Father Peter Miller, S.C.J., Provincial Superior.

The Recollect Augustinians are moving in this same direction. Of late they have been accepting as candidates only high school graduates, properly motivated, of course. They will be employed as soon as possible as teachers and prefects in the seminary. Another familiar trend is reflected in the recent admission of these brothers to recite part of the Office with the priests instead of the traditional "Our Fathers and Hail Marys."

In the Precious Blood Society brothers have no specific role; each is assigned to a position determined by his talents and the needs of the order. They will take an increasingly active part in the apostolate of the society, bringing Christ to the people through teaching, missionary work and the organizing of youth groups.

"In ten years I've seen a growth from a housekeeping and cooking apostolate to one of true diversification," writes Brother Dennis Mooney of the Conventual Franciscans. "As a brother in a clerical community, it is quite impossible to identify with a specific apostolate . . . and this is precisely an advantage to young men who do not have 'professional' aspirations." Franciscan Brothers have engaged in such varied studies as art at Catholic University and construction in community colleges. As their competence is demonstrated, their responsibility increases. "Limitations can be only those imposed by the brothers themselves," Brother Dennis continues. In all that he writes he simply demonstrates the Franciscan tradition that a man is a brother because of what he is rather than what he does.

On the other hand, the distant cousins of the Conventual Franciscans, the Franciscan Friars of the Atonement, expect their brothers to further the specific apostolate of the order and contribute to the Church unity movement. Their founder, Father Paul, anticipated today's ecumenical movement when he led his Anglican community into the Roman Communion in 1909. According to Brother Paschal Breau, Director of Brother Vocations, the order looks for intelligent persons who understand the purpose of the community. In the future brothers will engage in writing and will work more directly with lay people in the furtherance of the ecumenical movement.

The teaching brothers in the Congregation of the Holy Cross are an independent group, but there are over a hundred non-teaching brothers who remain part of the Holy Cross Fathers Congregation. The trend here as in so many other orders is away from manual and domestic work and toward "white collar" positions. Brothers receive degrees in Business Administration and attend secretarial and tailoring schools. According to Father Richard Sullivan, C.S.C., Provincial of the Eastern Province, the older on-the-job training has proven less satisfactory. Brothers have achieved a professional status with two college treasurers among them; another is the director of a food service institute for restauranteurs.

Similarly, there are Marist Brothers who are not members of the Marist Brothers of the Schools, but of the Marist Fathers. Confusing though this may be, the purpose is the same as in other clerical orders; they are expected to relieve the priests of the tasks which have little or nothing to do with the priest's ministry. Father Austin Verow, S.M., Provincial of the New England Province, mentions that brothers are sometimes sent to schools for practical nursing, and to community colleges for shop courses in industrial arts.

Brothers are co-workers in the White Fathers' African Missions. They spiritualize the same impulse which is leading thousands of other young Americans to Africa as part of the Peace Corps. Their work in teaching, in office and secretarial work, in directing agricultural work and modern workshops, in building roads, constructing churches, schools, hospitals and whole villages, is indispensable missionary work. Brother Louis Lacouture of Brockton, Massachusetts, for example, who specializes in carpentry in Kabale, Uganda, was called upon to construct an entire camp for four thousand war refugees. Father John Heigl, W.F., Vocation Director, foresees that more brothers will be engaged in teaching and other forms of youth work in Africa.

The same is true of the brothers in the Pontifical Institute for Foreign Missions, according to their Provincial, Father Nicholas Maestrini. Brothers work with priests in foreign missions as printers, mechanics, engineers and teachers. The emphasis is less on the status of assistant and more on that of a professional in his own right.

The Maryknollers have become one of the best known missionary societies in America, despite their rather recent origin. They were founded in 1911 by two American priests under the name of Catholic Foreign Mission Society of America. In addition to a thousand priests there are over two hundred brothers who engage in teaching and the various kinds of skilled labor required by mission work. An Associate of Arts program for teachers in Latin America has been started. Others take a two-year series of courses in a training institute, specializing in carpentry, masonry, automotive and electrical work. The fact that they are becoming so numerous indicates that the Maryknoll Brothers will assume a greater responsibility for the recruitment and training of new members.

Other orders repeat the same prognosis for their brothers:

Congregation of the Resurrection, "Increased apostolic work in educational and parochial fields."

Missionary Servants of the Most Holy Trinity, "A definite trend away from the use of the brother as a domestic or jack-of-all-trades."

Vincentians, "Until now our brothers have been of the lay state. I can see great possibilities in teaching and other fields."

Benedictines of St. Vincent, Latrobe, Pennsylvania, "More clerical work in offices as secretaries and even teachers. Days of domestic service are numbered."

Stigmatine Fathers, "In our last General Chapter, brothers were admitted to House Chapters for the purpose of discussing problems of the community. We hope that they may have a more active role in community and Church affairs."

Society of the Divine Word, "It is just coming into its own in this country. He will share more and more of the responsibility of the order and will thus free the priest for his ministerial duties."

Blessed Sacrament Fathers, "We expect that the usual brother will want to become proficient in some trade or occupation, that he will want the right to vote with the Fathers, that he will want to develop his education along the lines of the well-informed Catholic laymen."

Glenmary Missioners, "We shall probably lengthen their training program and very likely place more and more emphasis on specific training along the lines of their special talents. We expect them to be as perfect as possible witnesses for the non-Catholics of 'No Priest-Land, U.S.A.' "

Immaculate Heart Missioners, "We hope to use them more as procurators, managers, teachers and catechists."

Congregation of the Holy Ghost, "We have already tried to make the change from informal to formal training. This will enable the brother to assume a larger share of responsibility within the community."

Congregation of St. Joseph, "More brothers will be engaged in administrative roles."

Montfort Fathers, "More inclined to the apostolate; this will require a minimum training such as is given to members of the Confraternity of Christian Doctrine."

Congregation of Marian Fathers, "There is a greater desire on the part of our brothers to go into the teaching field and foreign missions."

Servants of the Holy Paraclete, "None except an improvement in their canonical status by amendment of our Constitutions to give them formal recognition. No brothers *de facto* are treated more as real brothers than ours."

Trinitarians, "Already our brothers are working side by side with us. Soon they will be praying the Divine Office with us."

Crozier Fathers, "Greater responsibility will be given to the brothers to manage the material part of the monastery and schools, teaching in seminaries and in Confraternity of Christian Doctrine programs."

Sacred Heart Missionaries, "True, they are being placed on a more equal plane with the Fathers than formerly when they had a subservient place—On the whole they will be better trained and educated."

Basilian Fathers, "Because of the extra work priests have to do today, the brother must be given more confidence and more responsibilities in the Church and monastery. I'm sure they will live up to this."

Passionists, "The role of the brother seems to be taking on a new look with possibilities of unlimited use especially in the changing apostolic role of the religious brother."

At this point I would imagine that the reader is groggy with quotes and overwhelmed by the litany of religious orders. He should also be convinced by the sheer weight of evidence that there is a massive *aggiornamento* working in all orders which include brothers. It is quite likely that the individuals in each order are unaware of the remarkable uniformity of the trend. There has been a radical readjustment of the brother's position vis à vis the priests within the last two decades. Gone is the notion that the priesthood was a higher grade of perfection; gone is the conscious class distinction. Today priest and brother are partners in the common enterprise. Of the two, the priest's activities are the more limited by reason of his ordination; he must do priestly work such as celebrating Mass, hearing confessions, and in general dispensing the sacraments. The brothers are the shock troops, not bound to one specific ministry. They can adapt to any new situation which confronts the order.

While we are on the subject of the various orders, it might be useful to note the qualifications looked for in candidates. We will mention just a few.

"We want men with a great desire for holiness expressed in a deep personal love for God and people." Fathers of the Sacred Hearts.

"Generous and dedicated individuals." Passionists.

"Humility, obedience, sincerity and co-operation." Basilians.

"Common sense, manliness, sincerity, initiative, daring, dedication." Croziers.

"Generous spirit, outgoing willingness to work, cheerfulness." Trinitarians.

"The three g's, godliness, graciousness, generosity." Servants of the Holy Paraclete.

"Qualities which would make the candidate versatile, since we want to use our brothers in all works where a priest who is ordained does not have to be." Marian Fathers.

"What every other order seeks, namely, character and moral virtues plus, good health and mind." Fathers of St. Joseph.

"High school diploma, balanced character, desire to serve God as a brother." Congregation of the Holy Ghost.

"Zeal, piety, commitment." Immaculate Heart Missioners.

"A sense of responsibility, docility, maturity and good health." Stigmatine Fathers.

"Adaptable, friendly, generous (spiritual, of course)." Jesuits.

"Health, spiritual and physical, desire and aptitudes. Generosity still gets top consideration." Maryknoll.

"Maturity, a religious (prayerful) spirit, intelligence." Holy Cross Fathers.

"Moral and physical qualities in common with just about everyone else. Specifically, men who are interested, who believe that work can be a means of salvation and 'preaching.'" Conventual Franciscans.

"For the future we want leadership qualities, capacity for higher education and/or technical training." Claretian Fathers.

To continue would be to repeat needlessly. Enough has been said to guide anyone who is reasonably aware of his own strengths and weaknesses. Almost all of the orders now require a high school diploma and good health as prerequisites. As for the rest, every skill and every talent finds an expression in the work of the brothers.

The same tendencies are at work among Anglican Brothers, who are smaller in numbers but otherwise almost indistinguishable from the Roman Catholic orders in organization and purpose. There is only one Anglican order exclusively for brothers, the St. Barnabas Brotherhood, founded in 1902 when Brother Gouverneur Provoost Hance with one novice began to live the religious life under the direction of a secular priest. His work was the operation of a convalescent home in downtown Pittsburgh. In 1908, a larger building was purchased at East McKeesport, Pennsylvania. The Founder and two brothers took perpetual vows in 1919 in the presence of Bishop Whitehead. The home was moved to Gibsonia, Pennsylvania in the same year. Today two homes for convalescent and incurable men and boys are maintained by the order, one is at Gibsonia, the other at North East, Pennsylvania.

The brothers' rule is modeled after the Benedictine. There is the usual period of postulancy, and a novitiate of two years, followed by two years of temporary vows and finally perpetual or "life" vows. The vows are the traditional ones, poverty, chastity, and obedience. The Eucharist is the central act of worship, and the usual monastic office is recited during the day.

The Society of St. Paul is primarily a lay community, but it does admit priests. The principal work of the Society is in geriatrics. Convalescent and nursing homes are in operation in Portland, Sandy, and Gresham, all in Oregon. Brothers are all trained in basic medical programs to the equivalent of Licensed Practical Nurse and General Lab Technician. They also receive training in physical therapy. Other brothers work in the field of publications or are involved in the Society's overseas medical mission program. The age requirement is higher than in other orders, candidates must be at least twenty-one and under forty. The other requirements are the usual endorsement by the parish priest, high school education, and freedom from serious financial or other encumbrances. According to Father René Bozarth, Rector, the future holds an expanded rehabilitation program in geriatrics and the staffing of an overseas home.

Other Anglican orders are clerical, but there is provision in each for the admission of brothers. Father Paul, Novicemaster of the Poor Brethren of St. Francis, whom we mentioned earlier in this work, writes that there are about as many brothers as there are priests, and practically no difference between them. The exception, of course, is that the priests administer the sacraments. All do manual work, all give retreats and conduct missions. All have seat, voice, and vote in Chapter and can hold office. These Franciscans seem to have achieved the equality which other orders are struggling toward.

Dom Anthony Damron, Subprior of Saint Gregory's Priory, Michigan, makes the same point. There are choir monks and lay-brothers among the Benedictines, but not all of the choir monks are ordained.

> Our lay-brothers happen to be so talented (shop work, clerical work, cooking, sewing) that no priests can take their place, but these works have just materialized as a result of the brothers' talents. They have the same training as the choir monks, even to studies . . .
>
> In the future we certainly see (along with other Benedictines) that the lay-brothers will be coming to most or all the offices and that they will have a seat at least at times on Chapter and surely they will be enabled to cast a vote for a new Abbot.

The Order of the Holy Cross is also a monastic community for priests and brothers. It was founded in 1884 in the slums of New York City's lower East Side by Father James Huntington. The Mother House and Novitiate are located in West Park, New York. The order conducts retreats for priests and laymen at the monastery and sends men out to do special preaching upon request. It also maintains an active publications department which turns out a monthly magazine as well as a number of books, tracts and pamphlets. In this ecumenical age, the white-clad monks from Holy Cross are frequent visitors to their Roman Catholic neighbors along the Hudson's "monastery row."

There are three branch houses of the order, a monastery at St. Andrew's School for Boys near Sewanee, Tennessee; Mount Calvary Retreat House in Santa Barbara, California; and a monastery at Bolahun in the interior of Liberia, West Africa, where the order carries on its overseas missionary work.

The oldest religious order for men in the Anglican Communion is the Society of Saint John the Evangelist, a community of priests and brothers known popularly as the Cowley Fathers. It was founded in 1866 in Cowley, England, by Father Richard Benson and two companions. The work of the order is essentially the same as so many others we have seen, the priests preach missions and conduct retreats, operate mission churches and serve as chaplains to sisterhoods. According to the rules of the Society,

> Lay Brothers may also be united with the Mission Priests in dedication to God in the religious state, and for assisting in whatever way they are able in the work of the Society, whose life they have been called to share, but the government of the Society shall reside with the professed Fathers only.

However, according to Father Alfred Pedersen, Superior of the Society, legislation is now in process which will soon give the lay brothers full Chapter rights. An unusual feature is that life vows cannot be taken before the age of thirty; brothers who enter over thirty must take temporary vows at least three years before perpetual profession.

The Oratory of the Good Shepherd was founded in Cambridge, England, in 1913 as "a society of unmarried priests and laymen in the Anglican Communion," but except for the earliest years there have been no laymen among them.

The same *aggiornamento* is at work among the Anglican orders as among the Roman Catholic. There is no doubt that the future will see a greater degree of co-operation among them, especially as the ecumenical movement brings the two churches more closely together. New insights into scriptural study, the dynamic liturgical renewal, and a new historical evidence on the delicate question of Roman recognition of the validity of

Anglican ordination are acting in concert to bridge the gap of four centuries.

The future will also see an expansion of monasticism among the Lutherans and other denominations, after the manner of the zealous Protestant monks of Taize, in France.

CHAPTER XII

The Converging Brotherhoods: A Lesson for Our Times

Other experiments in co-operation are necessary preliminary steps before there can be any significant inter-faith rapprochement. The first of these steps is the searching self-scrutiny each order of brothers must undergo to determine whether it is actually accomplishing its purpose. During the past ten years there have been conferences, workshops and studies within each order. Absolute candor and sincerity have characterized these sessions. Fundamental questions have been asked. Are our schools producing better Christians? With laymen assuming a more important role in the Church, are religious obsolete? Should brothers become priests? Would it not be better for an individual to be freed from the demands of institutional life in order to go out into the world where the important work waits to be done? Why have community exercises at all? What is our community?

Let us eavesdrop on some of the plain talk within the religious families, and at the same time hope that our presumption will be forgiven.

If names like Heidegger, Henrich Ott, Paul Tillich sound like those of German industrialists, or if Nedoncelle, Merleau-Ponty, Marcel, suggest new wave movie directors to us then we might wonder whether it really makes much difference what happened at Meriba. If the common market, control of

> nuclear weapons, the busing of school children seem the playthings of the editors of obscure magazines what's the point of a stress on regularity? Or, do we have that *inclusiveness* that Buber thinks to be the mark of the teacher, the ability to listen from the other side, so that we understand how students feel about the realities of the grades game, the discrimination and phoneyness that usually goes along with school athletics, their attitudes toward religious knowledge . . .

This was part of Brother Basil O'Leary's frank statement about community life, addressed to his fellow Christian Brothers and reprinted in their *Dialogue* of October 1964. In order to be competent, Brother O'Leary is saying, we need to remain abreast of the latest thinking in the meaning of the Christian message, we must become involved in the social crises of our times in that they are indeed our problems, we must re-evaluate the standard of values in our schools in order to use our resources in the most productive way for our students, our society and our Church. Discussions at the grass roots level are going on throughout the Christian Brothers world-wide community in preparation for their General Chapter.

The Marists are saying and doing the same thing. The keynote speaker at the Marist Educational Conference in November, 1963, reminded his fellow teachers that education is a discovery of oneself, and that a teacher must continue to grow into the fullness of his own personhood if he is to be able to assist the student in his own growth. Part of this growth is the admission that we are bound in a fellowship with people around us, and an acceptance of responsibility for problems which we did not create. To grow one must be alert to recognize values and sensitive enough to respond to them. To grow means to pursue knowledge ever more deeply until the distinction between secular and spiritual become blurred. Finally to become what we are is to discover the part a personal Christ plays in our lives. This last is the great reason for a separate school system, because public school teachers are not legally free to refer to this central fact of Christianity.

In 1963 the Marist Educational Committee established a special commission to study problems relative to adaptation in the life of a religious teacher. This study is part of a sweeping review of every aspect of Marist life, including the Constitutions of the order, in preparation for the General Chapter of the order in 1967, in Rome.

Among teaching orders the greatest attention is being given to the necessity for making the schools more effective. The manner in which the new learning can be reconciled to the spiritual life and the need to constructively harness the boundless energy and enthusiasm of the young men entering the religious life is being explored so that society may be better served.

Among the non-teaching brotherhoods similar conferences are going on and similarly frank questions are being asked. In a paper read to an international gathering of Franciscans at Vernay, Holland, in 1962, Father Cajetan Esser asked,

> What would happen, what will happen, to our Franciscan life, to our Franciscan communities without the presence of the brothers? Without the brothers our houses may well be reduced to mere "centers of action" for priests engaged in the apostolate, to a kind of "headquarters" (or home-base) for busy pastors of souls. Yet once this happens, once our convents come to lack what is a basic element of real community life, they will fail to give the harassed and hurried priest that quiet refuge he needs to maintain his peace of mind, that "family" to which he feels he belongs and in which he can recoup his losses and gain new strength. This means that our communities must never lack a certain element which

> gives them permanence—an element which is no less than the contemplative side of our life. To use the words of Saint Francis, we need both the "vita Marthae" and the "vita Mariae"; both are of mutual importance to Franciscans.

He called for a renewal of *fraternitas* or brotherhood, which was a characteristic of early Franciscans as it was of early Christians. His paper began a chain reaction which culminated in an historic first meeting of Franciscans of all orders of the North American continent on the subject of the Franciscan Brotherhood. The conference was held at St. Leonard's College, Dayton, Ohio, from April 3rd to the 6th, 1964.

> The window was indeed opened on this question and the fresh air of charity dusted off time-tested principles, as well as put new life into the brotherhood vocation—the full potential of which may yet be called upon to meet present needs of the Church.

Thus Father Augustine Hellstern summarized the proceedings in his preface to the report of the conference published in an attractive format for the perusal of all Franciscans.

In preparation for their General Congregation, the Jesuit Brothers circulated a report of a delightful conversation between a Brother Alfonso and the late Father Janssens, Father General of the order. Brother Alfonso very diplomatically pointed out that St. Ignatius had distinguished only between temporal and spiritual coadjutors in the Society, the first were brothers, the second priests. He had intended the two classes to be separated only during the training period, not in community. However, custom replaced the founder's wish and the more humble of the temporal duties were given to the brothers and the more dignified of the temporalities were reserved to priests. Brother Alfonso asked for a return to the spirit of St. Ignatius.

> I believe that this separation of classes must proceed from the old generations,

so reads the translation of Father Janssens' comments

> and perhaps it is also due to this that the separation of classes actually exists today in Europe and in Latin America where the Europeans have gone, continuing the custom with the same vigor with which it exists in Europe. Do not believe that this is so everywhere—And after all, Brother, I don't see anything unfitting in this fusion—

A meeting of Jesuit Brothers was held at Canisius College, Buffalo, from February 15th to the 17th, 1965 to discuss preliminaries to the General Congregation as they pertained to the status of the brothers in the Society. Ways were discussed of better utilizing brothers in the active apostolate. There was general agreement that contact be made with Cardinal Bea, a Jesuit, to petition the Council Fathers to define more clearly the vocation of the male religious who was not a priest. Portraying the new image of the brother to the American Catholics in general was the final, rather optimistic resolution of the meeting.

Thus at the present moment in the long history of brotherhoods there is more ferment, more huddling and questioning, more exciting possibilities, than in any other age.

It is almost inevitable that the next step will be toward greater co-operation among the various brotherhoods. There will be some mergers but the larger orders will retain their identities. There will be exchanges of personnel in the interests of greater efficiency. There will be joint experimental projects.

As evidence of the incipient program of co-operation a Brothers' Panel met at the Shoreham Hotel in Washington from September 28th to the 30th, 1964. The conference was the result of an earlier meeting of brothers from four different communities at the Precious Blood Mission House in Falls Church, Virginia in December of 1962. They discussed establishing a permanent organization which would embrace brothers of any and all societies and would exchange information on such aspects of the brother's life as methods of recruiting and training school techniques. The idea won widespread support from other brothers and received the endorsement of the President of the Conference of Major Superiors of Men in the United States. At their conference in July of 1964 the major superiors requested more information. A committee under Brother John Burney of the Precious Blood Congregation proceeded to draw up Constitutions and By-laws for an organization to be called simply "Brothers' Committee." There is no doubt that through this mechanism the co-operative movement will receive strength and direction. The committee will also be the means by which the new image of the brother will be presented to America, not as a member of a specific order but as "a brother."

Another important indication of co-operation is the *Brothers' Newsletter* which has already been referred to. The publication is both an effect and a cause of the movement. Significant also is the recent establishment of the Saint Joseph's Guild specifically for the purpose of promoting the brother's vocation. Basically, the Guild is a religious information center where all interested religious congregations are working together to introduce young men to the essential concept of the life and help guide them to the particular order which is best suited to their interests and aptitudes. Brother Francis Butler, a Jesuit, established the Guild when he realized how little the average boy knows about the opportunities and challenges of a brother's vocation. The Guild conducts monthly meetings for boys interested in the brother's life; it schedules tours of various monasteries and schools to enable them to see brothers at work. They are told that a brother works out his salvation in accordance with his abilities and the need of his community. Some brothers prefer teaching, others have surpassing skills in various trades. Some want to serve the sick, as medical technicians and doctors. Every talent, every skill, every good desire can be placed at the service of God among men. Literature from ninety-two different congregations is available at the Guild. The Guild makes use of the check-list which we have included in the Appendix as a guide to a young man in making his selection of the proper order.

The organization of the Brothers' Committee, the publication of the *Brothers' Newsletter* and the disinterested work of the St. Joseph's Guild are straws in the wind. If the rich personnel resources of the various brotherhoods can be efficiently co-ordinated we might predict that in the near future there will be studies, subsidized by the government or by private foundations, with the object of determining the resources of each of the brotherhoods. There will be an increase in the inter-change of personnel to the profit of all parties concerned. For example an academic administrator might spend a year or two in the college or school of another order in exchange for the services of a brother who is a qualified business manager or cafeteria director.

There is good reason to expect a breakthrough in the teaching apostolate. According to Marist Brother Martin Lang, in an article prepared for publication, there is an increasing emphasis on the teaching of religion within public universities. Today sixteen such institutions have Departments of Religion. There is every reason to believe that qualified brothers would be welcomed by the chairmen of these departments.

We might also predict that the brothers will assume a position of leadership in the nation-wide war against poverty. Social work has always been their forte, and now they are in a position to share their experience with newer workers in the field. They will be consultants in community action programs and in the work of public service organizations such as Vista. Their schools will become centers for the physical as well as moral rehabilitation of their neighborhoods.

The emphasis on excellence and the increasing professionalism in the work of the brothers will attract the more capable young men in the new generation. These "New Breeders" will have an unprecedented impact on the management of their various institutions, especially as they grow into positions of responsibility.

Young Americans will continue to become brothers, because they are idealistic and they are generous. One of Cardinal Suenens' remarks is true of them,

> A postulant is not principally drawn by the prospect of becoming a teacher or a hospital worker, rather he wants these activities to be the means whereby he might play his part in the salvation of the world.

The very existence of brothers is proof of the manliness of religion. They are visible witnesses to their fellow men of the resurrected life when temporal values will have disappeared in a consuming love of God. Brothers tell the world, as do priests and nuns, that sex is a fine and noble invention of the Creator but that its renunciation for the love of God in one's fellow men is noble also. All men have a need to love and be loved and whereas the father of a family naturally finds outlets for his affections in his wife and family, so the brother realizes his love within his community and his apostolate. Brothers who are highly competent psychologists and theologians are developing a philosophy of community, the art of living together.

Fraternal love is a very real fact of religious life. If this love can be clearly analyzed and adequately explained, then perhaps it can be communicated to a society whose greatest ache is loneliness, whose greatest need is love.

Appendix

For the convenience of those who want information about a specific order, below are listed all religious orders of men which include brothers with the name of the person to contact.

A.A.	ASSUMPTIONIST FATHERS Very Rev. Henri J. Moquin, A.A., Provincial Province of the U.S.A. and Canada 231 West 14th Street New York, New York 10011
S.A.	FRANCISCAN FRIARS OF THE ATONEMENT (Third Order Regular of St. Francis) General Motherhouse Graymoor Garrison, New York 10524
O.S.A.	AUGUSTINIAN FATHERS Very Rev. James G. Donnellon, O.S.A., Prior Provincial Province of St. Thomas of Villanova St. Thomas of Villanova Villanova, Pennsylvania 19085
O.R.S.A.	RECOLLECTS OF ST. AUGUSTINE Very Rev. Theophane Mayora, O.R.S.A., Prior Provincial

Province of St. Augustine
57 Ridgeway Avenue
West Orange, New Jersey 07052

O.S.B. BENEDICTINE FATHERS
Rt. Rev. Denis Strittmatter, O.S.B., Abbot Pres.
St. Vincent Archabbey
Latrobe, Pennsylvania 15650

ER. CAM. MONK HERMITS OF CAMADOLI
Very Rev. Dom Clement M. Roggi, Prior
New Camadoli
Big Sur, California 93920

S.S.S. CONGREGATION OF THE BLESSED SACRAMENT
Very Rev. Francis Costa, S.S.S., Provincial
Province of St. Ann
184 E. 76th Street
New York, New York 10021

O.S. CAM. CAMILLIAN FATHERS, or ORDER OF ST. CAMILLUS
Very Rev. M. Gilles, O.S. Cam., Provincial
North American Province
Camillian Provincialate
1611 S. 26th Street
Milwaukee, Wisconsin 53204

O.F.M. CAP. THE CAPUCHIN FATHERS
Very Rev. Thomas Janecek, O.F.M., Cap., Provincial
Province of St. Augustine
220 37th Street
Pittsburgh, Pennsylvania 15201

O. CARM. CARMELITE FATHERS
Very Rev. Aloysius Nagle, O. Carm., Provincial
Province of St. Elias
329 E. 28th Street
New York, New York 10016

C.M.F. CLARETIAN FATHERS, or MISSIONARY SONS OF THE IMMACULATE HEART OF MARY
Very Rev. Eugene N. Grainer, C.M.F., Provincial
Province of the East
400 N. Euclid Avenue
Oak Park, Illinois 60302

S.O. CIST. CISTERCIAN FATHERS
Rt. Rev. Raymond Molnar, S.O., Cist., S.T.D. Abbot
Our Lady of Spring Bank Cistercian Abbey
34639 W. Fairview Road
Oconomowoc, Wisconsin 53066

O.C.S.O. THE ORDER OF CISTERCIANS OF THE STRICT OBSERVANCE (Trappists)
Rt. Rev. M. James Fox, O.C.S.O., Abbot
Abbey of Our Lady of Gethsemani
Trappist P.O.
Kentucky 40073

O.C.D. DISCALCED CARMELITE FATHERS
Very Rev. Raymond Donoho, O.C.D., Provincial
Province of St. Therese of Oklahoma

	Monastery of Our Lady of Mt. Carmel and St. Therese 1125 S. Walker Street Oklahoma City, Oklahoma 73101
S.D.S.	SOCIETY OF THE DIVINE SAVIOR (Salvatorians) Very Rev. Jerome Jacobs, S.D.S., Provincial American Province Salvation Provincial Residence 1735 Hi Mount Boulevard Milwaukee, Wisconsin 53208
S.V.D.	SOCIETY OF THE DIVINE WORD Very Rev. Leo F. Hotze, S.V.D., Provincial Sacred Heart Province Divine Word Seminary Girard, Pennsylvania 16417
O.F.M.	FRANCISCAN FATHERS Very Rev. Sylvan R. Becker, O.F.M. Province of St. John the Baptist 1615 Vine Street Cincinnati, Ohio 45210
O.F.M. CONV.	CONVENTUAL FRANCISCANS (Friars Minor Conventual) Very Rev. David Schulze, O.F.M. Conv., Minister Provincial Province of the Immaculate Conception St. Francis Friary 812 N. Salina Street Syracuse, New York 13208

T.O.R. THIRD ORDER REGULAR OF ST. FRANCIS
Very Rev. Kevin R. Keelan, T.O.R., S.T.L.
Province of the Most Sacred Heart of Jesus
Provincial Residence
Loretto, Pennsylvania 15940

O.S.C. CANONS REGULAR OF THE ORDER OF THE HOLY CROSS (Crosier Fathers)
Very Rev. Benno Mischke, O.S.C., Provincial
Province of St. Odilia
R. 1, Wallen Road
Fort Wayne, Indiana 46805

C.S.C. PRIESTS OF THE CONGREGATION OF HOLY CROSS
Very Rev. Richard H. Sullivan, C.S.C., Provincial Superior
Province of Our Lady of Holy Cross
835 Clinton Avenue
Bridgeport, Connecticut 06604

M.S.F. CONGREGATION OF THE MISSIONARIES OF THE HOLY FAMILY
Very Rev. Henry Roemer, M.S.F., Provincial
4528 Maryland Avenue
St. Louis, Missouri 63108

C.S. SP. HOLY GHOST FATHERS
Very Rev. Vernon F. Gallagher, C.S.Sp., Ph.D.
Provincial
Eastern Province of the United States
915 Dorseyville Road
Pittsburgh, Pennsylvania 15238

THE GLENMARY HOME MISSIONERS
(The Home Missioners of America)
Very Rev. Clement F. Borchers,
Superior General
General Headquarters
The Glenmary Home Missioners
Cincinnati, Ohio 45246

S.J. JESUIT FATHERS
Rev. John G. Furniss, S.J.
Province of New York
39 E. 83rd Street
New York, New York 10028

M.I.C. MARIAN FATHERS
Very Rev. Ladislaus F. Pelczynski, M.I.C.,
Provincial Superior
St. Stanislaus Kostka Province
Eden Hill
Stockbridge, Massachusetts 01262

S.M. MARIST FATHERS
Very Rev. Austin E. Verow, S.M.
Boston Province
72 Beacon Street
Chestnut Hill, Massachusetts 02167

C.M.M. CONGREGATION OF MARIANNHILL MISSIONARIES, MARIANNHILL FATHERS
Very Rev. Reinald Hubert, C.M.M.,
Provincial
American Province
Our Lady of Grace Monastery
23715 Ann Arbor Trail
Dearborn, Michigan 48120

S.M.M. MISSIONARIES OF THE COMPANY OF MARY
(Montfort Fathers)
Very Rev. Roger M. Charest, S.M.M., Provincial
United States Province
101-18 104th Street
Ozone Park, New York 11416

S.M. SOCIETY OF MARY
(Marianists—Brothers of Mary)
Very Rev. John G. Dickson, S.M., Provincial Superior
Province of New York
Marianist Provincial House
2001 Providence Avenue
Chester, Pennsylvania 19013

O.M.I. OBLATES OF MARY IMMACULATE
Rev. Francis McCartin, O.M.I.
Our Lady of Hope Province
Oblate Novitiate
Tewksbury, Massachusetts

M.M. CATHOLIC FOREIGN MISSION SOCIETY OF AMERICA, INC. (Maryknoll)
Most Rev. John W. Comber, M.M., D.D., Superior General
Catholic Foreign Mission Society of America, Inc.
Maryknoll, New York

C.M. CONGREGATION OF THE MISSION
Very Rev. Sylvester A. Taggart, C.M., Provincial

Eastern Province of the U.S.A.
500 E. Chelten Avenue
Philadelphia, Pennsylvania 19144

S.A.C. SOCIETY OF THE CATHOLIC APOSTOLATE
(Pallottine Fathers)
Very Rev. Guido J. Carcich, S.A.C., Provincial
Province of the Immaculate Conception
309 North Paca Street
Baltimore, Maryland 21201

M.S. SS.T. MISSIONARY SERVANTS OF THE MOST HOLY TRINITY
Very Rev. Gerard P. Fredericks, M.S., SS.T., Custodian General
Holy Trinity Missionary Cenacle
9001 New Hampshire Avenue
Silver Spring, Maryland 20900

O.SS.T. THE ORDER OF THE MOST HOLY TRINITY
Very Rev. Daniel Giorgi, O.SS.T., Provincial
Immaculate Heart of Mary Province
Park Heights Avenue
Box 5742
Baltimore, Maryland 21208

C.O. ORATORIAN FATHERS
Very Rev. James J. Sharples, C.O., Provost
The Oratory of Rock Hill S.C.
P.O. Box 895
Rock Hill, South Carolina 29731

M.S. THE MISSIONARIES OF OUR LADY OF LA SALETTE

Very Rev. Michael J. Cox, M.S., Provincial
Eastern Province
Our Lady of Seven Dolors
120 Mountain Avenue
Bloomfield, Connecticut 06002

O.D.M. ORDER OF OUR LADY OF MERCY
Rev. James W. Esper, O.D.M., Superior
St. Raymond Nonnatus Seminary
LeRoy, New York 14482

C.P. CONGREGATION OF THE PASSION
Very Rev. Gerard Rooney, C.P., Provincial
Province of St. Paul of the Cross
St. Michael's Monastery
1901 West Street
Union City, New Jersey 07087

O.P. ORDER OF PREACHERS
Very Rev. Robert L. Every, O.P., Provincial
Province of St. Joseph
869 Lexington Avenue
New York, New York

C.PP.S. SOCIETY OF THE PRECIOUS BLOOD
Rev. H. V. Diller, C.PP.S.
Provincial Director of Missions and Retreats
American Province
1125 Harmon Avenue
Dayton, Ohio 45419

O.PRAEM. CANONS REGULAR OF PREMONTRE
(Norbertine Fathers)
Rt. Rev. Sylvester M. Killeen, O.PREAM., Abbot

	United States Circary St. Norbert Abbey 1016 N. Broadway De Pere, Wisconsin 54115
C.SS.R.	REDEMPTORIST FATHERS Very Rev. Ronald G. Connors, C.SS.R. Province of Baltimore 5 East 74th Street New York, New York 10021
C.R.	CONGREGATION OF THE RESURRECTION Very Rev. Bernard J. Bak, C.R., Superior Provincial Chicago Province 945 Sheridan Road Winnetka, Illinois 60093
M.S.C.	MISSIONARIES OF THE SACRED HEART Very Rev. Joseph W. Gaspar, M.S.C., S.T.D., Provincial United States Province Sacred Heart Monastery 305 S. Lake Street P.O. Box 270 Aurora, Illinois 60507
S.S.J.	ST. JOSEPH'S SOCIETY OF THE SACRED HEART (For Colored Missions) Very Rev. George F. O'Dea, S.S.J., Superior General 1130 N. Calvert Street Baltimore, Maryland

S.C.J.	CONGREGATION OF THE PRIESTS OF THE SACRED HEART Very Rev. Peter M. Miller, S.C.J., Provincial North American Province 407 Glenview Avenue Milwaukee, Wisconsin 53213
SS.CC.	FATHERS OF THE SACRED HEARTS Very Rev. Daniel J. McCarthy, SS.CC., Provincial North American Province 1 Main Street Fairhaven, Massachusetts 02719
O.S.B.M.	ORDER OF ST. BASIL THE GREAT Very Rev. Nicholas Kohut, O.S.B.M., Provincial American Province 22 East Seventh Street New York, New York 10003
P.S.S.C.	PIOUS SOCIETY OF THE MISSIONARIES OF ST. CHARLES Very Rev. Caesar Donanzan, P.S.S.C., Provincial Superior Province of St. Charles Borromeo Our Lady of Pompei Church 25 Carmine Street New York, New York 10014
S.S.E.	SOCIETY OF SAINT EDMUND Very Rev. Eymard P. Galligan, S.S.E., Superior General St. Joseph's Hall Winooski Park, Vermont 05404

O.S.F.S. OBLATES OF ST. FRANCIS DE SALES
Very Rev. John J. Conmy, O.S.F.S., Provincial
American Province
220 Kentmere Parkway
Wilmington 6, Delaware

O.S.J. OBLATES OF ST. JOSEPH
Very Rev. Andrew F. Porro, O.S.J., Provincial
Eastern Province
808 Susquehanna Avenue
West Pittston, Pennsylvania

S.S.P. PAULINE FATHERS
(Society of St. Paul for the Apostolate of Communications)
Very Rev. Stanislaus P. Crovella, S.S.P., Provincial
American Province
278 Warren Street
Brookline, Massachusetts 02146

S.D.B. SALESIANS OF ST. JOHN BOSCO
Very Rev. August P. Bosio, S.D.B., Provincial
Province of St. Philip the Apostle
148 Main Street
New Rochelle, New York 10802

O.S.M. SERVITE FATHERS (Servants of Mary)
Very Rev. Joseph M. Loftus, O.S.M., Provincial
Province of Our Lady of Sorrows
3111 West Van Buren Street
Chicago, Illinois 60612

C.P.S. STIGMATINE FATHERS
Very Rev. Charles F. Egan, C.P.S.,
Provincial Superior
North American Province
302 Maple Street
Springfield, Massachusetts 01105

O.S.B. SYLVESTRINE BENEDICTINES
Very Rev. Benedict Ferretti, O.S.B.,
Superior Major
St. Sylvester Monastery
17320 Rosemont Road
Detroit, Michigan 48219

W.F. WHITE FATHERS (Missionaries of Africa)
Very Rev. Anthony J. Coolen, W. F.
Provincial
United States Headquarters
1624 21st Street
Washington, D.C. 20009

C.I.C.M. IMMACULATE HEART OF MARY MISSION SOCIETY
Very Rev. Alphonse Rigouts, C.I.C.M.,
Provincial Superior
United States Province
P.O. Box BB
4651 N. 25th Street
Arlington, Virginia 22207

F.S.C.J. SONS OF THE SACRED HEART
(Verona Fathers)
Very Rev. Anthony Todesco, F.S.C.J.,
Provincial
United States Province

Sacred Heart Seminary
8108 Beechmont Avenue
Cincinnati, Ohio 45230

P.I.M.E. PONTIFICAL INSTITUTE FOR FOREIGN MISSIONS
Very Rev. Nicholas Maestrini, P.I.M.E., Provincial Superior
United States Province
121 E. Boston Boulevard
Detroit, Michigan 48202

C.S.J. CONGREGATION OF ST. JOSEPH
Rev. Julius Parise, C.S.J., Vice-Provincial
P.O. Box 1704
Albuquerque, New Mexico 87103

I.M.C. CONSOLATA SOCIETY FOR FOREIGN MISSIONS (Consolata Fathers)
Very Rev. Ambrose N. Ravasi, Regional Superior
P.O. Box 365, Lincoln Highway
Somerset, New Jersey 08873

O. CART. ORDER OF CARTHUSIANS
Rev. Stephen M. Boylan, O. Cart., Pres.
Carthusian Foundation
Arlington, Vermont 05250

M.H.M. MILL HILL MISSIONARIES
(St. Joseph's Society for Foreign Missions of Mill Hill)
Very Rev. Peter Heymans, M.H.M., Superior
American Headquarters
Mill Hill
Albany, New York 12203

s.P. SERVANTS OF THE HOLY PARACLETE
Very Rev. Gerald M. C. Fitzgerald, s.P., Servant General
Via Coeli
Jemez Springs, New Mexico 87025

O.S.P. PAULINE FATHERS
Rev. Lucius Tyrosinski, O.S.P., Prior
United States Headquarters
Pauline Fathers Monastery
P.O. Box 151, Iron Hill and Ferry Roads
Doylestown, Pennsylvania 18901

M.Sp.S. MISSIONARIES OF THE HOLY GHOST
Rev. Charles Furber, M.Sp.S., Superior
St. Martha's Church
4433 Santa Fe Avenue
Los Angeles, California 90058

M.Ss.A. MISSIONARIES OF THE HOLY APOSTLES
Very Rev. Eusebe M. Menard, O.F.M., Superior General
1335 Quincy Street, N.E.
Washington, D.C. 20017

C.R.S. SOMASCHAN FATHERS
(Order of St. Jerome Aemilian)
Rev. Cesare De Santis, C.R.S., S.T.L., Litt. D. Superior
St. Jerome Aemilian Hall
628 Hanover Street
Manchester, New Hampshire

Membership in the following orders is limited to brothers, no priests are included.

C.F.A.	ALEXIAN BROTHERS Bro. Flander Renaud, Provincial Superior United States Province 1200 W. Belden Avenue Chicago, Illinois 60614
F.C.	BROTHERS OF CHARITY Bro. Emeric Rigney, F.C., Delegate American District House 7720 Doe Lane Philadelphia, Pennsylvania 19118
F.S.C.H.	CHRISTIAN BROTHERS OF IRELAND Bro. William C. Penny, Provincial American Province for the United States 21 Pryer Terrace New Rochelle, New York 10800
F.I.C.	BROTHERS OF CHRISTIAN INSTRUCTION (La Mennais Brothers) Rev. Bro. Henry G. Vanasse, F.I.C., Provincial American Province Notre Dame Institute Alfred, Maine 04002
F.I.C.M.	BROTHERS OF THE IMMACULATE HEART OF MARY General Motherhouse P.O. Box 77 Old Washington, Ohio

F.S.C. BROTHERS OF THE CHRISTIAN SCHOOLS
Bro. Charles Henry, F.S.C.
Assistant to the Superior General for the American Provinces
330 Riverside Drive
New York, New York

O.S.F. FRANCISCAN BROTHERS OF BROOKLYN
Bro. Bertrand Ryan, O.S.F., Superior General
General Motherhouse
41 Butler Street
Brooklyn, New York 11231

F.F.S.C. FRANCISCAN BROTHERS OF THE HOLY CROSS
Bro. Michael, Superior
American Branch
St. James Trade School
R.R. No. 1
Springfield, Illinois 62707

O.S.F. FRANCISCAN MISSIONARY BROTHERS OF THE SACRED HEART OF JESUS
Rev. Bro. David Irza, O.S.F., Superior
Motherhouse
R.R. 3, Box 39
Eureka, Missouri 63025

O.H. HOSPITALLER ORDER OF ST. JOHN OF GOD
Very Rev. Bro. Christopher Azzolino, O.H., Vicar Provincial

	American Vice-Province of Our Lady Queen of Angels St. John of God Hospital 2035 W. Adams Boulevard Los Angeles, California 90018
C.S.C.	BROTHERS OF THE CONGREGATION OF THE HOLY CROSS Bro. John W. Donoghue, C.S.C., Provincial Eastern Province of the Brothers of the Holy Cross 24 Ricardo Street West Haven, Connecticut 06516
F.M.S.	THE MARIST BROTHERS Rev. Bro. Philip Robert, F.M.S., Vocational Director Province of Esopus P.O. Box 186 Esopus, New York 12429
F.M.M.	BROTHERS OF MERCY Rev. Bro. Gabriel McGrath, F.M.M. Provincial Superior St. John of God Province Sacred Heart Home 4520 Ransom Road Clarence, New York 14031
S.C.	BROTHERS OF THE SACRED HEART Provincial House Province of New York R.D. #1, Box 215 Belvidere, New Jersey 07823

C.F.P. BROTHERS OF THE POOR OF ST. FRANCIS
Rev. Bro. Matthew Lyons, C.F.P., Provincial Superior
Province of St. Joseph
Mt. Alverno School
Price Hill
Cincinnati, Ohio 45238

C.F.X. BROTHERS OF ST. FRANCIS XAVIER
Ven. Bro. Gilroy, C.F.X., Provincial
St. Joseph Province
601 Winchester Street
Newton Highlands, Massachusetts 02161

M.M. MARYKNOLL AUXILIARY BROTHERS, CATHOLIC FOREIGN MISSION SOCIETY OF AMERICA, INC.
(Maryknoll Brothers)
Most Rev. John W. Comber, M.M., Superior General
Maryknoll, New York 10545

B.G.S. BROTHERS OF THE GOOD SHEPHERD
Bro. Matthias, Director General
General Motherhouse
P.O. Box 352
Albuquerque, New Mexico 87103

BROTHERS OF SAINT PIUS X
Rev. George Passehl
General Motherhouse
Box 438
DeSoto, Wisconsin 54624

F.S.E. BROTHERS OF THE HOLY EUCHARIST
Bro. Aloysius Scafidi, Superior General
R.F.D. 2, Box 283
Bunkie, Louisiana 71322

F.S.R. BROTHERS OF THE HOLY ROSARY
(Congregation of Our Lady of the Rosary)
General Motherhouse and Novitiate
101 Boynton La.
Reno, Nevada 89502

S.F.C. CONGREGATION OF THE BROTHERS OF CHARITY OF THE IMMACULATE HEART OF MARY
Motherhouse and Novitiate
Villa Maria
1067 W. Gilman Street
Banning, California 92220

B.C.S. BROTHERS OF CHARITY OF SPOKANE
Rev. Eugene Mulligan,
Superior and Novice Master
R.R. 1, P.O. Box 383
Colbert, Washington 99005

F.S.J. BROTHERS OF ST. JOSEPH
Bro. Joseph Levesque, Superior
P.O. Drawer 248
Bethany, Oklahoma

F.S.P. BROTHERS OF ST. PATRICK
(Patrician Brothers)
Bro. Cornelius, F.S.P., Superior
St. Patrick's Novitiate
7820 Bolsa Avenue
Midway City, California 92655

Religious orders of men, Protestant Episcopal Church.

S.C.C.	SOCIETY OF THE CATHOLIC COMMONWEALTH Father Superior, S.C.C. Oratory of St. Mary and St. Michael 52 Olive Street Newburyport, Massachusetts
C.S.S.S.	CONGREGATION OF THE COMPANIONS OF THE HOLY SAVIOUR Rev. Robert L. Ducker, C.S.S.S. St. Martin's Church Lumberton, New Jersey
	ORATORY OF THE GOOD SHEPHERD (American College) Rev. H. Martin P. Davidson (Prior of the American College) St. John's Church Frostburg, Maryland
	ST. BARNABAS' BROTHERHOOD Brother Superior St. Barnabas' House Gibsonia, Pennsylvania
O.S.B.	ORDER OF ST. BENEDICT Father Prior, Very Rev. Dom Benedict Reid, O.S.B. St. Gregory's Priory Rt. 3, Priory Road Three Rivers, Michigan

O.S.F.	ORDER OF ST. FRANCIS Rev. Father Minister, O.S.F. Little Portion Mount Sinai, Long Island, New York
S.S.J.E.	SOCIETY OF MISSION PRIESTS OF ST. JOHN THE EVANGELIST The Rev. Father Superior, S.S.J.E. 980 Memorial Drive Cambridge 38, Massachusetts
B.S.P.	THE BROTHERS OF ST. PAUL Bro. Robert Paul Allan, B.S.P., Director St. George's House Bracebridge, Ontario Canada
	SOCIETY OF ST. PAUL Father Rector P.O. Box 446 Gresham, Oregon
O.H.C.	ORDER OF THE HOLY CROSS Father Superior, O.H.C. West Park, New York

Check list for prospective brothers.

Years of High School ________ Years of College ________

Are you interested in a particular community of Brothers? ____

____

Do you prefer teaching exclusively? ________________

Have you a special interest for teaching in Grammar School?

____

High School? ________________ College? ______________

Do you prefer hospital work, as a medical technician or doctor?

____

Do you prefer monastic life (e.g., Trappist)? ______________

Do you speak, read or understand a foreign language? ________

Specify: __________________________________

Have you had any schooling in a trade? __________________

Specify: __________________________________

If you do not know a trade, would you like to learn one? _____

Specify your preference: __________________________

Do you have a special hobby? ______________________

Do you prefer work in the United States? ________________

Are you interested in foreign service (e.g., Africa, South America, Japan)? __________________________________

For service in the United States as a Brother, do you have a preference for work in a particular locality: New England, Southeast, Southwest, Far West, North Central? ____________

Do you have a preference for a specialty in work (e.g., publishing, radio and communications, missions among the hill and backwoods people, among the Negroes, among the Indians?) Specify: ____

____

Additional remarks: ____________________________

____

____

____

____

Your name ______________________ Age __________

Address ____

____

Brother Director
St. Joseph Guild
39 East 83rd Street
New York, New York 10028
Telephone BU 8-6200, Area Code 212

Bibliography

Burns, C.S.C., J. A., and Kohlbrenner, Bernard J., *A History of Catholic Education in the United States,* New York, Benziger Brothers, 1937.

Burton, Katherine, *Chaminade, Apostle of Mary,* Milwaukee, The Bruce Publishing Company, 1946.

Canu, Jean, *Religious Orders of Men,* New York, Hawthorn Books, 1960.

Ellis, John Tracy, *American Catholicism,* University of Chicago Press, 1955.

Goebel, Edmund J., *A Study of Catholic Secondary Education During the Colonial Period up to the First Plenary Council of Baltimore, 1852,* New York, Benziger Brothers, 1937.

Kane, George L., *Why I Became a Brother,* Westminster, Maryland, The Newman Press, 1964.

Maher, S.J., Trafford P., *Lest We Build on Sand,* New York, The Catholic Hospital Association, 1962.

O'Leary, Bro. K. Basil, "The Brother," *Commonweal,* 23 April 1965.

Probst, George (ed.), *The Happy Republic,* New York, Harper and Brothers, 1962.

Ready, O.F.M., Gabriel, *Secular Institutes,* New York, Hawthorn Books, 1962.

Schleck, Charles A., *The Theology of Vocation,* Milwaukee, The Bruce Publishing Co., 1962.

Thomas, F.M.S., Bro. Martin, *The Historical Growth and Development of the Marist Brothers in the United States,* Marist College Press, 1961.

Tyler, Alice Felt, *Freedom's Ferment,* New York, Harper and Row Publishers, 1944.

Life of Marcellin Joseph Benedict Champagnat, by One of His First Disciples, Paris, Desclee and Co., 1947.

The Guidepost, A Religious Vocation Manual for Young Men, Compiled by the Catholic University Conference of Clerics and Religious of the Catholic Students Mission Crusade, 1953.

Additional Reading Material

Adelbert James, Bro., "Brotherhood, in Fact," *Extension,* v. 42, p. 31, January 1948.

Albright, T., "What is a Benedictine Brother?" *St. Joseph Magazine,* v. 65, p. 7-9, April 1964.

"Brothers of the Christian Schools," *America,* v. 79, p. 3, April 10, 1948.

Anselm, Bro. E., "Brother's Vocation," *National Catholic Education Association Proceedings,* v. 46, p. 304-307, 1949.

August Raymond, Bro., "Christian Brothers in the U.S.," *Lasallian Digest,* v. 2, p. 3-23, Spring 1960.

Breau, P., "What is a Brother?", *Lamp,* v. 59, p. 16-17, April 1961.

"Hospitaller Brothers of St. John of God," (abridged), *Catholic Digest,* v. 12, p. 63-67, August 1948.

Celestine Luke, Bro., "The Theology of the Brother's Vocation," *Lasallian Digest,* v. 3, p. 68-81, Spring 1961.

Dumas, B., "The Formation of High School Students in Juniorates," *Franciscan Educational Conference,* v. 44, p. 141-150, 1963.

Everett, M. F., "Charity Unlimited," *Voice of St. Jude,* v. 21, p. 6-9, August 1955.

Greiner, F., "Christ's Career Men," *Catholic School Journal,* v. 64, p. 38-40, March 1964.

Gutierrez, A., "Teaching Brothers in Christ," *Review for Religious,* v. 20, p. 257-264, July 1961.

Hael, I., "Lay Brothers I Have Known," *Pax,* v. 27, p. 130-132, September 1937.

Hakenewerth, Q., "Why Brothers Don't Become Priests," *American Ecclesiastical Review,* v. 144, p. 14-22, January 1961.

Hakenewerth, Q., "Clarification of the Brother Vocation," *National Catholic Education Association Bulletin,* v. 59, p. 497-500, August 1962.

Janning, J., "Brothers, We Go Places," *Shield* (College Ed.), v. 33, p. 11-12, March 1954.

John XXIII, Pope, Address to Major Superiors of the Brothers of the Christian Schools: the vocation of the teaching brother, (June 14, 1961), *Lasallian Digest,* v. 3, p. 4-7, Summer 1961.

Jude, Fr., "Here's How Johnny Became a Brother," *Catholic Home Journal,* v. 50, p. 9, March 1950.

Kelley, F. C., "Nursing Orders: their origin and needs," *America,* v. 72, p. 89, November 4, 1944.

Kelty, C., "Some Observations on Brothers," *Catholic Mind,* v. 47, p. 735-740, December 1949.

Kerr, J., "Jesuit Brother," *Catholic Digest,* v. 14, p. 50-52, January 1950.

Kramer, H. G., "Father Chaminade and the Christian Brothers," *La Sallian Digest,* v. 3, p. 40-44, Summer 1961.

Lord, D., "The Religious Brother," *La Sallian Digest,* v. 2, p. 38-41, Spring 1960.

Luke Joseph, Bro., "Apostolate of the Working Brother," *La Salle Catechist,* v. 26, p. 126-32, Spring 1960.

McArdle, P., "The Lay Brother's Vocation," *Doctrine and Life,* v. 13, p. 420-24, August 1963.

McCluskey, J., "The Marianist Mission," *Marianist,* v. 52, p. 45-50, April 1961.

Martin, Bro. D., "Brothers, the Church, and Waste," *Catholic School Journal,* v. 48, p. 81-82, March 1948.

Mathias, Bro., "Lay Brotherhood Devoted to Care of the Sick and Poor," *Hospital Progress,* v. 18, p. 52-53, February 1937.

Pius XII, Pope, "High Mission of the Teaching Brother," *Pope Speaks,* v. 1, p. 125-127, July 1954.

Sauvage, Bro. M., "The Teaching Brother in the Church," *La Sallian Digest,* v. 4, p. 34-47, Fall 1961.

"Brethren of the Common Life," *Sign,* v. 26, p. 51, April 1947.